# GRAMMAR IN ACTION 3
## An Illustrated Workbook

Barbara H. Foley
Deborah Singer Pires
Elizabeth R. Neblett

**HEINLE & HEINLE PUBLISHERS**
*A Division of Wadsworth, Inc.*
*Boston, Massachusetts 02116*

Director: Laurie E. Likoff
Full-Service Manager: Michael Weinstein
Production Coordinator: Cynthia Funkhouser
Text and Cover Design: A Good Thing, Inc.
Text Illustrations: Agustin Fernandez and Bill Ogden
Production: PC&F, Inc.
Printer and Binder: Malloy Lithographing, Inc.

GRAMMAR IN ACTION 3: An Illustrated Workbook

Library of Congress Cataloging-in-Publication Data

(revised for vol. 3)

Foley, Barbara H.
    Grammar in action.

    Vol. 3 by Barbara H. Foley, Deborah Singer Pires,
and Elizabeth R. Neblett.
    1. English language—Textbooks for foreign speakers.
2. English language—Grammar—1950—  —Problems,
exercises, etc. I. Dowling, Gretchen.    II. Title.
PE1128.F56  1990        428.2'4        89-23021
ISBN 0-8384-2750-2

To Gretchen Dowling
8/31/43–4/13/89

A gifted teacher.
A natural writer.
A special friend.

# CONTENTS

# INTRODUCTION

*Grammar in Action 3* is the third in a series of three grammar workbooks for young adult and adult ESL/EFL students. It is geared to intermediate-level students and for those students who may not have a strong background in formal grammar. Designed to capture students' interest, each unit is centered about a real-life situation or problem. The situation is introduced by a picture and, in many units, a short text read by the teacher. The picture and text create a context for the lesson, introduce vocabulary, and clarify the meaning and context of language. Approximately eight exercises follow, four oral and four written. The final exercise in each chapter is a reading passage that includes the target structure and that contrasts verb tenses. Grammar reference pages provide clear charts of the grammatical forms, as well as simple explanations of meaning and usage.

## WORKBOOK FEATURES

This workbook is for **intermediate-level students** and for those students who have had little formal grammar. In *Grammar in Action 3* only one grammatical item is covered per unit, and it is presented in small, well-sequenced increments. Considerable practice on each point is provided. Each context is pictured so that new vocabulary and meaning are always clear and concrete. Finally, simple grammatical charts and explanations are included at the end of each unit. These are intended as reference only and may be used at any time in the unit.

Each unit centers about a **context,** that is, a picture of a relevant situation or problem. In many units, there is also a Teacher Text. The students look at the pictures and the teacher reads the Teacher Text, found at the back of the book. These sentences explain the sequence of actions or give additional information about the illustrations. The pictures and text are designed to enable the students to recount the story or information. Furthermore, the other exercises within the units are all related to the context. The grammar exercises cannot be done mechanically, simply by filling in a word. Correctness of the grammar is tied to the accuracy of the statement so that the grammar is seen as meaningful.

The book includes a **variety of exercises.** The exercises are carefully sequenced to guide students from a general introduction to meaningful use of the grammar. The exercises are designed to teach, not to test. They help the students visualize and figure out the grammatical pattern under discussion, as well as grasp its meaning. Additionally, the varied exercises require the students to perform different tasks. This allows for individual differences in learning styles and prevents "mechanical" completion of exercises.

Finally, the book is a **versatile teaching tool.** It can be adapted to numerous teaching styles and aims. The exercises may be manipulated in groups, individually, or as a whole class. The lessons may be used "as is," or the pictures and contexts may act as springboards for free conversation, dialog creation, dictation, or other forms of creative interaction.

# THE UNITS

Each unit in the workbook follows the same format: **picture, exercises, reading passage, and grammar reference charts.**

The **picture** is the core of the unit: all vocabulary, meaning, and grammar emerge from it. As the unit begins, the class should talk about the picture and what they see happening. Some students may simply wish to give a vocabulary word or a simple sentence. Other students at this level will be able to construct a complete scenario.

Accompanying many of the Units is a Teacher Text at the back of the book. Each is a series of ten or more sentences that give further information about the pictures; most of the sentences use the target structure. The teacher reads the sentences in a natural voice while the students look at the picture. Depending upon the level of the class, this reading may be repeated three or more times. After the students clearly understand the context and vocabulary, they try to retell the information about one or more of the pictures. Some students may have questions about the grammar and its usage. The exercise allows the students to hear and recognize the new structure before it is presented in print.

The teacher should also encourage students to volunteer other information, opinions, or personal experiences related to the situation. Brief cultural explanations may be made if necessary. The focus of this preliminary discussion is to generate student interest and to clarify meanings, not to correct grammar.

In the body of the unit, there are both **speaking and writing exercises.** The speaking exercises familiarize the students with the vocabulary and grammar of the unit. Typically, the students might be asked to read statements about the picture to decide if they are true or false, or to match a sentence and a picture. Each unit includes a chart, used to form sentences or questions about the picture. The charts help the students visualize the pattern of the structure and include all the elements of the grammar in their sentences.

Several units ask the students to choose the correct form of the verb. Most speaking sections conclude with a series of questions about the situation.

The speaking exercises are instructional and clear. They give examples, show patterns, help students distinguish between two choices, and include prompt boxes. They are designed to teach the grammar and to provide the students with increasing grammatical awareness. There are many ways to utilize the speaking exercises in *Grammar in Action 3*. Depending on the students' proficiency and the teacher's personal style, the exercises may be used whole class, in small groups, or individually.

The writing exercises provide an opportunity for the students to work alone or in pairs. These exercises are contextualized. Students are directed to fill in sentences with the correct word, to choose the correct form of a word, to form questions, or to answer questions about the context. The writing exercises may be used as an in-class assignment or as homework. In the first few units, it will be necessary to do several examples of each exercise together as a class. Once the students are familiar with the written assignments, they will not need this support. All written exercises should be corrected in class. During this time, the teacher can answer questions and further assess the students' understanding of the grammar.

A reading passage related to the context follows the exercises. The passage is not restricted to the target structure; other intermediate verb tenses and structures are included. After they read the story, the students answer inference questions, which involve a more complete understanding of the material. The reading activity also serves as a verb contrast activity, presenting material and asking questions with a variety of structures.

The final activity in most units is a section entitled "Discussion Questions." These questions encourage the students to talk about their own experiences and ideas related to the context of the lesson. The questions may be discussed either in a class or in small groups. Some of the students' answers and experiences could be expanded into short compositions.

At the conclusion of each unit are one or more **grammar boxes** outlining the grammar included in the unit. The grammar boxes are not taught or memorized, but are provided as a reference. When using them, it is helpful to have the students read sentences from the boxes. Students then can be encouraged to give other examples from the unit they are studying or from their own lives.

# IN CONCLUSION

*Grammar in Action 3* is a grammar workbook. The picture contexts are the starting points. The exercises then provide clear and thorough grammar practice. Additionally, teachers will want to use these units as springboards for directed discussions, free conversations, dialog activities, and other creative interactions. The teachers can use the students' language to expand the units and to meet the interests and needs of their particular ESL/EFL classes.

# ACKNOWLEDGMENTS

The faculty at the Institute for Intensive English, Union County College, remained constant, supportive, and helpful throughout this project. Our thanks to the teachers and students who experimented with various units in their classes and provided suggestions.

Special thanks to Marinna Kolaitis, who always remained calm and cheerfully encouraging. She was the final arbitrator on all grammar discussions.

Several individuals provided us with information on processes and careers:

Katherine Dupuis delineated a few typical settlements in divorce cases. Joseph Haedrich had an audience for his several trips to wine country. Lily Kliman helped us understand the role of the art therapist. Jo Romine outlined the job titles and responsibilities in the accounting field. Karen Suisa described the day-to-day operation of a jewelry store. Donald Trinks explained the arrest process and the workings of the National Crime Information Center.

# GRAMMAR IN ACTION 3

## UNIT 1
# THE CLASS

## Present Continuous with Who

**A.** Look at the picture and listen to your teacher talk about the class. Write the correct name for each picture. After you listen twice, talk about each person.

| | | |
|---|---|---|
| Ana | Harry | Paulo |
| Azra | Jorge | Roberto |
| Celio | Katarina | Tina |
| Ravi | Marie | Toshi |
| Françoise | Mario | |

**B.** Use the chart. Ask and answer questions about the class.

**Example:** What is Toshi listening to?

| What | | Katarina | doing? |
| | | Roberto | holding? |
| Where | is | Toshi | listening to? |
| | | | drinking? |
| Who | are | Tina and Marie | wearing? |
| | | Ana and Paulo | talking to? |
| Why | | Ravi and Azra | standing? |
| | | | sitting? |
| | | | sleeping? |
| | | | coming in late? |

**C.** Look at the picture. Read each statement. Circle "T" if it is true. Circle "F" if it is false.

| | | |
|---|---|---|
| 1. The student who is sitting next to the window is listening to music. | T | (F) |
| 2. The student who is bouncing the basketball is a baseball player. | T | F |
| 3. The student who is drinking a soda is a photographer. | T | F |
| 4. The students who are coming in late are wearing fashionable clothes. | T | F |
| 5. The student who is looking in his dictionary is a shoe salesman. | T | F |
| 6. The student who is sitting near the door is reading a book. | T | F |
| 7. The students who are writing on the blackboard are wearing sneakers. | T | F |
| 8. The person who is sitting under the clock is the ESL teacher. | T | F |
| 9. The student who is wearing headphones is listening to music. | T | F |
| 10. The students who are wearing uniforms are talking to the teacher. | T | F |

**D.** Combine these two sentences with **who**. Then, answer the question.

**Example 1:** Who's that woman? She's sitting by the window.

Who's that woman? ⟨Who⟩ ~~She~~'s sitting by the window.

*Who's that woman who is sitting by the window? That's Katarina.*

**Example 2:** Who are those students? They're wearing fashionable clothes.

Who are those students? ⟨Who⟩ ~~They~~'re wearing fashionable clothes.

*Who are those students who are wearing fashionable clothes?*
*They're Ana and Paulo.*

1. Who's that man? He's looking in his dictionary.

2. Who's that man? He's listening to music.

3. Who's that man? He's sleeping.
4. Who's that woman? She's drinking a soda.
5. Who are those students? They're sleeping.
6. Who are those people? They're coming in late.
7. Who are those students? They're writing on the blackboard.
8. Who's that man? He's sitting under the clock.
9. Who's that student? He's bouncing a basketball.
10. Who are those students? They're wearing white uniforms.

## Writing

**A.** Complete these questions about the class.

1. Who *is bouncing a basketball* ?
   Roberto is.

2. What _____ ?
   He's listening to rock music.

3. Where _____ ?
   She's sitting next to the window.

4. Who _____ ?
   Ana and Paulo are.

5. Why _____ ?
   Because their bus was late.

6. Who _____ ?
   They're talking to Harry.

7. What _____ ?
   His dictionary.

8. Why _____ ?
   Because they're tired.

9. What _____ ?
   They're wearing fashionable clothes.

10. What _____ ?
    They're writing sentences.

**B.** Complete these sentences with the correct form of the verb.

| | | | |
|---|---|---|---|
| bounce | listen | sleep | is |
| come | look | talk | are |
| drink | sit | write | |

1. The man who *is sitting* under the clock *is* the ESL teacher.

2. The students who _____ in late _____ models.

3. The student who _____ a soda _____ a photographer.

4. The student who_____ a basketball _____ a basketball player.

5. The students who_____ on the blackboard _____ baseball players.

6. The student who _____ in his dictionary _____ a shoe salesman.

7. The students who _____ _____ engineers.

8. The student who_____ by the window_____ an ice skater.

9. The student who _____ to music _____ a rock musician.

10. The students who _____ to the teacher _____ nurses' aides.

**C.** Combine these sentences with **who.**

**Example:** The woman is a photographer. She's from France.

The woman is a photographer. She's from France.
*The woman who's from France is a photographer.*

1. The students are baseball players. They're from the Dominican Republic.

*The students who are from the Dominican Republic are baseball players.*

2. The woman is an ice skater. She's sitting next to Françoise.

_____

3. The student is a rock musician. He's from Osaka, Japan.

_____

4. The student is a shoe salesman. He's from Rome, Italy.

_____

5. The students are models. They're from São Paulo, Brazil.

_____

6. The student is a basketball player from Cuba. He's very tall.

   _____

7. The women are from Haiti. They're wearing white uniforms.

   _____

8. The woman is an engineer from Yugoslavia. She's sleeping.

   _____

9. The person is an ESL teacher from Ohio. He's sitting at the desk.

   _____

10. The student is an engineer from India. He's sleeping.

    _____

**D.** Complete the conversations about the students in the lounge. Use your imagination to add some interesting information.

1. Tom: Who's that woman?

   Mike: Which one?

   Tom: The one _who is talking on the phone_ .

   Mike: That's _Janet_ . She's a _computer science major_ .
   She's from _California_ .

2. Tom: Who's that woman?

   Mike: _____ ?

   Tom: The one who _____ .

   Mike: That's _____ . _____ ?

6

3. Tom: Who's that woman?

Mike: _____ ?

Tom: The one who _____ .

Mike: That's _____ . _____ .

4. Tom: Who's that woman?

Mike: _____ ?

Tom: The one who _____ .

Mike: That's _____ . _____ .

5. Tom: Who's that woman?

Mike: _____ ?

Tom: The one who _____ .

Mike: That's _____ . _____ .

## Grammar Summary

| The student | who is drinking a soda | is | a photographer. |
|---|---|---|---|
| The students | who are studying English | are | nurses. |

The student is a rock musician. *Who* He's listening to music.
*The student who is listening to music is a rock musician.*

### Question:

Who is that student **who is listening to music?**
**Note:** Generally in speaking, *who is = who's.*

### Who Questions–subject:

Who **is sitting** next to Ravi?          Toshi is.
Who **is talking** to Harry?          Tina and Marie are.

### Who Questions–object:

Who **is** Ravi **sitting** next to?          To Toshi.
Who **are** Tina and Marie **talking** to?          To Harry.

# THE DIVORCE

## Future Going to

**A.** Look at the pictures and listen to your teacher talk about Amy and Tom's divorce. After you listen two or three times, retell the story.

**B.** Read each sentence. Write the number of the matching picture on the line.

_____ a. Tom is going to pay alimony.

_____ b. Tom is going to move to another town.

_____ c. Amy is going to get a job.

_____ d. Tom and Amy are going to divide their savings.

_____ e. The children are going to visit their father once a month.

_____ f. Amy is going to keep the house.

_____ g. The children, Carly and Tyrone, are going to live with their mother during the school year.

_____ h. Tom and Amy are going to get a divorce.

_____ i. Amy is going to study accounting part-time in the evenings.

_____ j. Tom is going to rent a small apartment.

**C.** Use the chart. Ask and answer questions about the divorce.
   **Example:** Is Tom going to pay child support? **Yes, he is.**

| Yes, he/she is. | Yes, they are. |
| No, he/she isn't. | No, they aren't. |

| | | | | |
|---|---|---|---|---|
| Is | Tom<br><br>Amy | going to | keep<br><br>get<br><br>pay<br><br>live | the house?<br>a job?<br>a divorce?<br>alimony?<br>child support?<br>in another town?<br>with their mother?<br>with their father?<br>in the same house? |
| Are | the children | | | |

**D.** Answer these questions about the pictures.

1. Who is going to keep the house?
2. Who are the children going to live with?
3. What is Amy going to study?
4. When is Amy going to study?
5. How often are the children going to visit their father during the school year?
6. When is Tom going to move?
7. Where is he going to live?
8. Is Tom going to pay child support?
9. When are the children going to live with their father?
10. What are Tom and Amy going to do with their savings?

## Writing

| Divorce Agreement | |
|---|---|
| **Tom** | **Amy** |
| Child support: $100 a week | Keep house |
| Alimony:  $75 a week for three years | Pay mortgage and taxes |
| 1990 Toyota | 1985 Ford |
| $7,000 in savings | $7,000 in savings |
| Keep television, VCR, stereo | Keep furniture |
| Pay for college for Tyrone | Pay for college for Carly |
| Medical bills for the children | Get own medical insurance |
| Pension | |

| Children | |
|---|---|
| Father -  summer<br>        first weekend of each<br>            month<br>        Thanksgiving | Mother - school year<br>        Christmas |

**A.** Complete these sentences with the correct form of the verb.

| | | |
|---|---|---|
| divide | live | take |
| keep | pay | visit |

1. Tom *is going to pay* child support.

2. Carly and Tyrone _____ with their mother during the school year.

3. Tom _____ the Toyota.

4. The children _____ their father the first weekend each month.

5. Tom and Amy _____ their savings.

6. Tom _____ $75 a week alimony for three years.

7. Amy _____ the Ford.

8. Carly and Tyrone _____ with their father in the summer.

9. Amy _____ the mortgage on the house.

10. Tom _____ the television with him to his new apartment.

**B.** Complete these questions about the divorce agreement.

1. When *are* the children *going to live* with their father? In the summer.

2. How much child support _____ Tom _____ ? $100 a week.

3. Who _____ the stereo system? Tom is.

4. Which car _____ Amy _____ ? The 1985 Ford.

5. How much alimony _____ Tom _____ ? $75 a week.

6. How long _____ Tom _____ alimony? For three years.

7. Who _____ the mortgage? Amy is.

8. How often _____ the children _____ their father? Once a month.

9. How _____ Tom and Amy _____ their savings? 50/50

10. Who _____ college costs for Tyrone? Tom is.

**C.** Life is going to be very different for the Larson family. Change these sentences to the future negative and use **anymore**.

1. Tom comes home for dinner.

   *He isn't going to come home for dinner anymore.*

2. The family eats dinner together.

   _____

3. The children see their father everyday.

   _____

4. Their father reads to them every night before they go to bed.

   _____

5. Tyrone and Carly live with their mother and father.

   _____

6. The family takes a vacation together in the summer.

   _____

7. Tom lives in Plainfield.

   _____

8. Tom comes home to his family after work.

   _____

9. Amy stays home all day.

   _____

10. Amy is home when the children get home from school.

   _____

**D.** Read this story. Then, answer the questions.

Amy is looking through her closet. What should she wear for the interview tomorrow? A new dress? Pants and her favorite pink top? A pair of jeans and a sweater? Tomorrow is her first job interview.

There is an opening for a custodian in the local school system. Amy knows she can do the work, sweeping, mopping floors, emptying the garbage, cleaning the girls' locker rooms. The salary is $10 an hour, and the benefits are excellent. But all the other custodians are men. How is the supervisor going to feel about hiring a woman? Is he going to give her a chance?

Amy is also worried about her children. The job is from 8:00 A.M. to 4:00 P.M. Amy can drop the children at school on her way to work. But when they get home from school, no one will be there. Can they stay by themselves for an hour? What is she going to do when one of the children is sick?

1. Where is Amy?

   _____

2. What is she looking for?

   _____

3. What job is she applying for?

   _____

4. How many women custodians are there?

   _____

5. Is Amy worried that the work is too difficult?

   _____

6. How is Amy going to feel after a day at work?

   _____

7. Why is this a good job for Amy?

   _____

8. Who is going to take the children to school?

   _____

9. Why is Amy worried about the children?

   _____

10. Amy is not sure she is going to get the job. Why?

    _____

## Discussion Questions:

1. Do you know anyone who is divorced?
2. Did they hire a lawyer?
3. Does the couple have any children?
4. Whom do the children live with? How often do they see the other parent?
5. Are the husband and wife still friendly?
6. How have their lives changed since the divorce?
7. How did they divide their belongings?
8. Why do people get divorced?
9. In your country, is there alimony or child support?
10. In the story, Amy is applying for a job as a custodian, which is usually a man's job. What do you think about this?

# Grammar Summary

## Statements:

| I | am | | |
|---|---|---|---|
| You We They | are | going to get | a job. |
| He She It | is | | a divorce. |

## Yes/No Questions:

**Is** Tom **going to pay** alimony?   Yes, he **is**
**Are** they **going to get** a divorce?   Yes, they **are**.

## Wh Questions:

Where **is** Tom **going to live**?   In another town.
When **is** he **going to move**?   Tomorrow.

## Simple Present

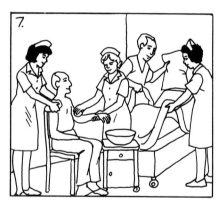

**A.** Patty is the head nurse at General Hospital. Look at the pictures and listen to your teacher read about her daily routine. After you listen two or three times, retell the information.

**B.** Read each sentence. Write the number of the matching picture on the line.

———— a. The nurses feed the patients.

———— b. Patty supervises the nurses on the fourth floor.

———— c. Patty listens to the night nurse's report on tape.

———— d. Patty gives medications.

———— e. The nurses wash the patients.

———— f. Patty checks the IVs.

———— g. The nurses make the beds.

———— h. The night nurse leaves her report on the tape recorder.

———— i. The nurses take the temperature and blood pressure of their patients.

———— j. Patty writes her assignments.

**C.** Read each statement. Circle "T" if it is true. Circle "F" if it is false.

| | | |
|---|---|---|
| 1. When Patty first comes into the hospital, she looks in on the patients. | (T) | F |
| 2. The night nurse hands Patty her report. | T | F |
| 3. Patty listens to the tape and writes the assignments. | T | F |
| 4. The nurses wash the patients. | T | F |
| 5. The nurses take the temperature and blood pressure of their patients. | T | F |
| 6. Patty doesn't feed the patients. | T | F |
| 7. The nurses feed all of the patients at lunchtime. | T | F |
| 8. Patty supervises the other nurses. | T | F |
| 9. All the nurses give medications. | T | F |
| 10. Patty checks the IVs. | T | F |

**D.** Circle the correct form of the verb.

1. Patty **check / checks** the IVs.
2. The nurses **make / makes** the beds.
3. Patty **write / writes** the assignments.
4. The nurses **take / takes** the temperatures.
5. Patty **listen / listens** to the night nurse's report.
6. Patty **give / gives** medications.
7. The nurses **wash / washes** the patients.
8. The nurses **feed / feeds** the patients.
9. Patty **read / reads** the doctors' orders.
10. Patty **check / checks** the patients.

**E.** Use the chart. Ask and answer questions about Patty's work.

**Example:** Do the nurses make the beds? **Yes, they do.**

| Does | Patty | check the patients?<br>listen to the night nurse's report?<br>write the assignments?<br>read the doctors' orders? |
|---|---|---|
| Do | the nurses | feed the patients?<br>wash the patients?<br>make the beds?<br>give medications? |

Yes, she does.
No, she doesn't.

Yes, they do.
No, they don't.

## Writing

**A.** Complete these sentences with the correct form of the verb.

| assign | feed | listen to | read | wash |
|---|---|---|---|---|
| check | give | make | take | |

1. Patty _*checks*_ the IVs.

2. She _____ the night nurse's report on tape.

3. She _____ duties to the other nurses on the floor.

4. The nurses _____ the beds.

5. They _____ the patients.

6. Patty _____ the doctors' orders.

7. Patty _____ the medications.

8. The nurses _____ the temperatures.

9. They _____ the blood pressure.

10. The nurses _____ the patients at lunchtime.

**B.** Complete these questions about the picture with **Do** or **Does.** Then answer each question.

1. *Does* Patty check the patients when she comes in? *Yes, she does.*

2. _____ the night nurse tell Patty her report?_____

3. _____ Patty check the doctors' orders?_____

4. _____ the nurses make the beds?_____

5. _____ the patients take their medications themselves?_____

6. _____ the nurses feed the patients at 3:00? _____

7. _____ Patty feed the patients? _____

8. _____ Patty take the patients' temperatures? _____

9. _____ the patients take their own blood pressure?_____

10. _____ Patty supervise the other nurses? _____

**C.** Complete these **Who** questions. Then, answer the questions with **do** or **does.**

1. Who *checks* the IVs?                          Patty *does* .

2. Who _____ the doctors' orders?          Patty _____ .

3. Who _____ the beds?                     The nurses _____ .

4. Who _____ the patients their medications?  Patty _____ .

5. Who _____ some of the patients at lunchtime?  The nurses _____ .

6. Who _____ the patients' temperatures?   The nurses _____ .

7. Who _____ Patty her report?             The night nurse _____ .

8. Who _____ to the tape?                  Patty _____ .

9. Who _____ the patients in the morning?  The nurses _____ .

10. Who _____ the duties?                  Patty _____ .

**D.** Read the answer. Then, write the question about Patty and her work.

1. Where _does Patty work_ ? At General Hospital.

2. Which _____ ? The 4th floor.

3. What _____ ? She's a head nurse.

4. What _____ ? The night nurse's report.

5. When _____ ? After she listens to the tape.

6. What _____ ? The IVs.

7. What _____ ? Their medications.

8. What _____ ? They feed some of the patients.

9. When _____ ? In the morning.

10. What else _____ ? They take their temperature and blood pressure.

**E.** Read the story. Then, answer the questions.

## PATTY

Patty is a nurse. She has a hard job because she works in the hospice unit of a large hospital. The people in her ward know that they will die. They have diseases that cannot be cured. Patty likes her job because she helps patients and makes them more comfortable. She checks her patients everyday when she comes in. She comes into their rooms with a bright smile and a cheerful voice. She says "Good morning," and she has a conversation with them while she takes their vital signs. Sometimes her patients can't talk at all. Sometimes her patients complain about the difficult night they had. They tell her about their aches and pains. Mostly, they are happy to see her. Sometimes they talk about the past. Often they talk about their fears. Patty listens. She knows she has an important job. It's difficult for the patients to talk to their families about death. They don't want to upset the people who love them. But Patty is not a member of the family. So they feel comfortable with Patty, and they talk about dying. Patty is a good listener. She thinks that's one of the most important parts of her job. Even though she doesn't like to get too friendly with her patients, she always does. And she always feels sad when they die. She has a hard job.

1. Where does Patty work?

   _____

   _____

2. What's wrong with her patients?

   _____

   _____

3. How does Patty feel about her job?

   _____

   _____

4. What's the first thing Patty does when she arrives?

   _____

   _____

5. How does she greet her patients?

   _____

   _____

6. What does she do while she takes their temperature and blood
   pressure?

   _____

   _____

7. What do her patients talk about?

   _____

   _____

8. Why don't Patty's patients talk to their families about death?

   _____

   _____

9. Why doesn't Patty like to get friendly with her patients?

_____

_____

10. Why is Patty's job difficult?

_____

_____

## Grammar Summary

The simple **present tense** describes routine actions.

### Statements:

| I<br>You<br>We<br>They | feed<br>don't feed | the patients. |
|---|---|---|
| He<br>She<br>It | checks<br>doesn't check | |

### Yes/No Questions:

| Do | I<br>you<br>we<br>they | check | the patients? |
|---|---|---|---|
| Does | he<br>she<br>it | | |

| Yes, | I<br>you<br>we<br>they | do. |
|---|---|---|
| No, | | don't. |
| Yes, | he<br>she<br>it | does. |
| No, | | doesn't. |

**Wh Questions:**

| | |
|---|---|
| When **does** she **check** the patients? | Every morning. |
| When **do** they **feed** the patients? | At breakfast and lunch. |

**Who Questions:**

| | |
|---|---|
| Who **works** at General Hospital? | Patty does. |
| Who **works** at General Hospital? | The nurses do. |

# THE JEWELRY STORE

## Present with Before and After

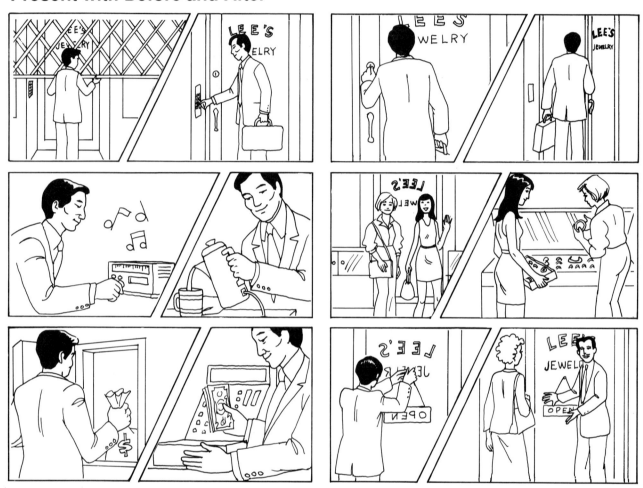

**A.** Look at the pictures and listen to your teacher talk about Lee. Lee owns a small jewelry store in the Waterside Shopping Center. Before the customers arrive, he has many things to do. After you listen two or three times, retell the story.

**B.** Circle the correct word.

1. **Before** / **After**   the customers arrive, Lee has many things to do.
2. **Before** / **After**   Lee arrives, he rolls up the gate.
3. **Before** / **After**   he rolls up the gate, he turns off the alarm.
4. **Before** / **After**   he enters the store, he unlocks the door.
5. **Before** / **After**   he makes a pot of coffee, he turns on the radio.

6. **Before / After**   his employees arrive, Lee takes the money from the safe.

7. **Before / After**   his employees arrive, they unlock the storage cabinets.

8. **Before / After**   his employees unlock the storage cabinets, they put the jewelry in the showcase.

9. **Before / After**   the customers enter, Lee puts the "Open" sign on the door.

10. Lee turns off the alarm **before / after** he rolls up the iron gate.

11. Lee turns on the radio **before / after** he makes a pot of coffee.

12. Lee makes a pot of coffee **before / after** his employees arrive.

13. His employees have a cup of coffee **before / after** they arrive.

14. Lee counts the money **before / after** he puts it in the cash register.

15. Lee puts up the Open sign **before / after** he puts the money in the cash register.

**C.** Use the chart. Form sentences about the picture.

**Example:** After Lee opens the store, he has a lot to do.

|  | | | | |
|---|---|---|---|---|
| After<br><br>Before | Lee | arrives,<br>opens the store,<br>rolls up the iron gate,<br>turns off the alarm,<br>enters the store,<br>unlocks the door,<br>turns on the radio, | he | has a lot to do.<br>rolls up the iron gate.<br>turns off the alarm.<br>unlocks the door.<br>enters the store.<br>makes a pot of coffee.<br>takes the money out<br>of the safe. |

**D.** Answer these questions. Use **before** or **after** in your answer.

**Example:** When does Lee put the Open sign on the door?
    He puts it on the door **after** he puts the money in the cash register.

1. When does Lee roll up the iron gate?

2. When does he turn off the alarm?

3. When does he enter the store?

4. When does he turn on the radio?

5. When does he make a pot of coffee?

6. When do his employees arrive?

7. When do Linda and Karen unlock the storage cabinets?

8. When do they display the jewelry trays?

9. When does Lee take the money out of the safe?

10. When do the customers arrive?

**E.** Answer these questions about your own schedule.

1. What time do you get up?
2. What do you do after you get up?
3. What do you do after you eat breakfast?
4. What do you do before you leave your house in the morning?
5. What do you do before you come to school?
6. What do you do after you arrive at school?
7. What do you do after your class is over?
8. What do you do after you get home?
9. What do you do before dinner?
10. What do you do before you go to sleep?

## Writing

**A.** Complete these sentences with the correct form of the verb.

| arrive | display | make | roll | turn on |
|--------|---------|------|------|---------|
| come | enter | put | take | unlock |

1. Lee _rolls_ up the gate after he _arrives_ at the store in the morning.

2. He _____ up the gate before he _____ the store.

3. Before he _____ the store, he _____ the door.

4. Before he _____ a pot of coffee, he _____ the radio.

5. Lee _____ a pot of coffee before his employees _____.

6. Linda and Karen _____ out the jewelry trays after they _____ the cabinets.

7. They _____ the jewelry after they _____ it from the cabinets.

8. Lee _____ the money out of the safe after his employees _____.

9. He _____ it in the cash register after he _____ it out of the safe.

10. Lee _____ the Open sign on the door before his customers _____ in.

**B.** Combine these sentences in two different ways. Use **after** in the first sentence. Use **before** in the second sentence.

**Example:** Lee counts the money. Lee puts the money in the cash register.

    a. *After Lee counts the money, he puts it in the cash register.*

    b. *Lee counts the money before he puts it in the cash register.*

1. Lee turns off the alarm. Lee unlocks the door.

    a. _____

    b. _____

2. Lee unlocks the door. Lee enters the store.

    a. _____

    b. _____

3. Lee turns on the radio. Lee makes a pot of coffee.

    a. _____

    b. _____

4. Lee makes coffee. His employees arrive.

    a. _____

    b. _____

5. Lee puts the money in the cash register. He puts the Open sign on the door.

    a. _____

    b. _____

**C.** Lee always closes the jewelry store with the same routine. Write ten sentences about the pictures below with **before** or **after.**

| lock | put up | count | put |
| turn off | leave/lock again | roll down | drive |

1. *Before Lee puts up the Closed sign, he locks the door.*

2. _____ .

3. _____ .

4. _____ .

5. _____ .

6. _____ .

7. _____ .

8. _____ .

9. _____ .

10. _____ .

**D.** Read the story. Then, answer the questions.

### KAREN

Even though Karen only works at Lee's Jewelry Store part-time, she is exhausted when she goes to sleep. She is always running. She never has one moment for herself. She has a thousand things to do everyday. Why? Because Karen is a working mother. Her day doesn't end when she leaves work. It just begins. After she leaves the store, she picks up her son, David, from school and drops him off at home. Then she picks up her daughter from a different school and drives her to her piano lesson. While Sara is at her piano lesson, Karen stops by the supermarket. Before she goes home, she picks up Sara. When she gets home, she prepares dinner and helps the children with their homework. Next, she serves dinner, prepares lunches for the next day, and clears the kitchen table before her husband gets home. Her husband works late every night. When he gets home, they both give the children a bath. Then, he goes downstairs to have dinner, and Karen reads the children a story before she puts them to bed. After that, she spends a few minutes talking with her husband before she takes a shower. Finally, they both relax in bed and watch the 11:00 news. Before he turns off the light, her husband always asks, "Well, dear, did you do anything today?"

1. Does Karen work at Lee's Jewelry Store from 9:00 to 5:00?

_____

2. How does she feel by the time she goes to bed?

_____

3. Describe Karen's day.

_____

4. At approximately what time does Karen leave Lee's Jewelry Store?

_____

5. What does Karen do after she picks up her daughter, Sara?

_____

6. What does Karen do while she prepares dinner?

_____

7. When does she read the children a story?

_____

8. What time do you think her husband comes home?

_____

9. How often does Karen's husband come home at 5:00?

_____

10. What does Karen do before she goes to sleep?

_____

## Discussion Questions:

1. Are you (Is someone you know) a working mother?
2. Describe your day.
3. Would you rather stay home with the children?
4. How long have you been doing this?
5. Were you working before you had children?
6. Did you take time off to have children?
7. Does your husband help you with the children and with the housework?
8. Why do you think most women work?
9. Should women work when their children are young? What's your opinion?

## Grammar Summary

A time clause begins with words such as **before** and **after.** A time clause has a subject and a verb. In the present tense, both the verb in the main clause and the verb in the time clause are in the present tense.

Lee turns on the radio.                  He makes a pot of coffee.

| Main Clause | Time Clause |
|---|---|
| He makes a pot of coffee | after he turns on the radio. |
| He turns on the radio | before he makes a pot of coffee. |

| Time Clause | Main Clause |
|---|---|
| After he turns on the radio,* | he makes a pot of coffee. |
| Before he makes a pot of coffee, | he turns on the radio. |

**\*Note:**  When the time clause is first, use a comma to separate it from the main clause.

**Past**

A. Look at the pairs of pictures. Listen to your teacher talk about life in Colonial times and life today. After you listen two or three times, retell the information.

**B.** Read each statement about Colonial Times.  Circle "T" if it is true. Circle "F" if it is false.

| | | |
|---|---|---|
| 1. People went to the supermarket. | T | (F) |
| 2. People had electric lamps. | T | F |
| 3. People cooked on open fires. | T | F |
| 4. People milked their own cows. | T | F |
| 5. People drove cars. | T | F |
| 6. People talked to their friends on the telephone. | T | F |
| 7. Most Colonial schools had one room. | T | F |
| 8. People made their own clothes. | T | F |
| 9. People watched television. | T | F |
| 10. People slept on mattresses and box springs. | T | F |

**C.** Circle the correct verb.

1. Colonial people **watched / didn't watch** television.
2. Colonial people **grew / didn't grow** their own food.
3. Colonial people **milked / didn't milk** cows.
4. Colonial people **drove / didn't drive** cars.
5. Colonial people **wrote / didn't write** letters.
6. Colonial people **made / didn't make** their own clothes.
7. Colonial women **cooked / didn't cook** over open fires.
8. Colonial children **studied / didn't study** in one-room schoolhouses.
9. Colonial people **used / didn't use** candles for light.
10. Colonial people **slept / didn't sleep** on mattresses.

**D.** Form sentences about Colonial times with **used to.** Use the pictures and follow the example.

**Example:** Today many people buy milk in supermarkets.
In Colonial times people used to milk their own cows.

1. Today most people buy food in supermarkets.
   (vegetables)

2. Today many people sleep on mattresses.
   (feather beds)

3. Today many women buy clothes in department stores.
   (own clothes)

4. Today most people cook on gas or electric stoves.
   (over open fires)

5. Today many people have electric lamps.
   (candles)

6. Today most people use oil or gas for heat.
   (wood)

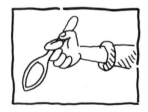

7. Today most people eat with forks, knives, and spoons.
   (spoons and their fingers)

8. Today most people drink from plastic or glass containers.
   (wooden mugs)

9. Today most people wear coats in the winter.
   (cloaks)

10. Today some people go to church every week, but others never go.
    (almost everyone)

**E.** There are 12 things wrong with this picture about Colonial times. Can you find them?

**Examples:** Children didn't play with toy trucks.
Houses didn't have air conditioners.

## WRITING

**A.** Complete these sentences with the correct form of the verb. Some of the sentences are negative.

| buy | read | watch |
|---|---|---|
| cook | sleep | wear |
| grow | study | write |
| have | use | |

1. Colonial people _____ *grew* _____ their own food.

2. Colonial people _____ *didn't buy* _____ milk at stores.

3. Colonial people _____ on gas stoves.

4. Colonial people _____ over open fires.

5. Colonial people _____ electricity.

6. Colonial people _____ candles for light.

7. Colonial people _____ letters to their friends.

8. Colonial people _____ telephones.

9. Colonial families _____ books to each other.

10. Colonial families _____ television.

11. Colonial children _____ in large modern schools.

12. Colonial children _____ in one-room schoolhouses.

13. Colonial families _____ on feather beds.

14. Colonial families _____ on mattresses and box springs.

15. Colonial girls _____ miniskirts.

**B.** Answer the questions with **used to.** Use the vocabulary in the box to help you answer the questions.

| cows | open fires | wooden houses |
|---|---|---|
| pipes | horses and wagons | leather boots |
| wooden wheels | long skirts | own clothes |
| | one-room schoolhouses | |

1. Did Colonial people live in apartment buildings?

No, they didn't. *They used to live in wooden houses* .

2. Did Colonial children wear sneakers?

No, they didn't. _____ .

3. Did Colonial men drive cars?

No, they didn't. _____ .

4. Did Colonial families buy milk at grocery stores?

No, they didn't. _____ .

5. Did Colonial girls wear miniskirts?

No, they didn't. _____ .

6. Did Colonial vehicles have tires?

No, they didn't. _____ .

7. Did Colonial children study in modern school buildings?

No, they didn't. _____ .

8. Did Colonial women cook on barbecue grills?

No, they didn't. _____ .

9. Did Colonial women shop at department stores for their clothes?

No, they didn't. _____ .

10. Did Colonial men smoke cigarettes?

No, they didn't. _____ .

**C.** Complete the questions about Colonial times.

1. What *did Colonial people grow* ? Vegetables.

2. Where _____ ? In small wooden houses.

3. What _____ ? Long skirts.

4. How _____ ? By horse and wagon.

5. Where _____ ? In one-room schoolhouses.

6. What kind of _____ ? Feather beds.

7. Where _____ ? Over open fires.

8. What _____ for light? Candles.

9. What _____ ? Boots.

10. What _____ on Sunday? They went to church.

**D.** Read the story and answer the questions.

### PLYMOUTH, MASSACHUSETTS

Every year thousands of people take summer vacations. Last year many people went to Plymouth, Massachusetts. The most popular tourist attraction is Plimouth Plantation. At the plantation, actors pretend to live and talk like the residents of the early colony. Visitors also see the ship *Mayflower,* which the Pilgrims sailed from England to America in search of religious freedom. Another popular historical sight is Plymouth Rock. When the Pilgrims came to America in 1620, they landed there.

At first, many people are surprised when they see Plymouth Rock. It is very small—much smaller than they had expected. For many years, visitors used to take pieces of the rock home as souvenirs. The Pilgrim Society was afraid the rock would soon disappear, so they moved the rock to a different place and put a fence around it.

1. What attractions are popular in Plymouth, Massachusetts?

_____

2. Do real Pilgrims live on Plimouth Plantation?

_____

3. What is the *Mayflower?*

_____

4. How did the Pilgrims get to America?

_____

5. Where did the Pilgrims come from?

_____

6. Why did the Pilgrims leave England?

_____

7. Why are many visitors surprised when they see the rock?

_____

8. How big is Plymouth Rock?

_____

9. Why is the rock so small?

_____

10. What protects the rock today?

_____

## Discussion Questions:

Is there a historical site near you? Tell the class about it.

# Grammar Summary

## Statements:

| I<br>You<br>We<br>They<br>He<br>She<br>It | used<br>didn't use<br><br>had<br>didn't have | candles.<br>electricity.<br>cars.<br>horses and wagons. |
|---|---|---|

## Yes/No Questions:

| Did | I<br>you<br>we<br>they<br>he<br>she<br>it | use<br><br>have | electricity?<br><br>candles? |
|---|---|---|---|

| Yes, | I<br>you<br>we<br>they | did. |
|---|---|---|
| No, | he<br>she<br>it | didn't. |

## Wh Questions:

| Where **did** they **live**? | In wooden houses. |
| What **did** Colonial girls **wear**? | Long skirts. |

# UNIT 6
# THE ROBBERY

## Past, Simple Time Clauses

**A.** Look at the pictures and listen to your teacher tell the story about the robbery at Lee's jewelry store. After you listen two or three times, retell the story.

**B.** Read each statement. Look at the pictures. Circle "T" if it is true. Circle "F" if it is false.

|  |  |  |  |
|---|---|---|---|
| 1. | Spike put on his gloves after he broke the window. | T | (F) |
| 2. | Spike climbed into the store after he broke the window. | T | F |
| 3. | As soon as Spike stepped onto the floor, the police arrived. | T | F |
| 4. | Before Spike left the store, he grabbed some jewelry. | T | F |
| 5. | After he jumped out of the window, the alarm rang. | T | F |
| 6. | When he got out of the store, he heard the police siren. | T | F |
| 7. | As soon as he saw the police, he ran down the alley. | T | F |
| 8. | Before Tina could drive away, the police caught her. | T | F |
| 9. | Before Spike could climb over the wall, the police grabbed his foot. | T | F |
| 10. | After the police caught Spike, he broke the store window. | T | F |

**C.** Use the chart. Make sentences about the story.

| | |
|---|---|
| Before Spike got out of the car,<br>After Spike broke a window,<br>As soon as Spike stepped onto the floor,<br>After he picked up the jewelry,<br>When he got out of the store,<br>As soon as he saw the police car,<br>When the police arrived,<br>When the police saw Spike,<br>Before he climbed over the wall,<br>Before the police took Spike and Tina to<br>    the police station, | he jumped out of the window.<br>he put on gloves, a mask, and a hat.<br>he climbed into the store.<br>Tina tried to drive away.<br>the police grabbed his foot.<br>the alarm rang.<br>he heard a police siren.<br>they put handcuffs on them.<br>they chased him.<br>Spike ran down an alley. |

**D.** Answer the questions about the robbery.

**Example:** When did Spike climb into the store?
      **After he broke the window**

1. What did Spike do before he got out of his car?
2. What did Spike do before he climbed into the store?
3. What happened as soon as Spike stepped onto the floor?
4. What did Spike do before he left the store?
5. When did the police arrive?
6. When did Tina try to drive away?
7. When did Spike begin to run?
8. When did the police chase Spike?
9. When did the police catch Spike?
10. What did the police do when they caught Spike and Tina?

## WRITING

**A.** Complete these sentences with the correct word. In some sentences more than one answer is correct.

| | |
|---|---|
| after | before |
| as soon as | when |

1. Spike put on gloves _before_ he got out of the car.

2. Spike broke the window_____ he climbed into the store.

3. Spike climbed into the store _____ he broke the window.

4. The alarm rang _____ Spike stepped onto the floor.

5. Spike grabbed some jewelry _____ the alarm rang.

6. _____ he jumped out of the window, he grabbed some jewelry.

7. The police came _____ the alarm rang.

8. Spike began to run _____ he heard the police siren.

9. _____ the police saw Spike, they chased him.

10. Tina tried to drive away _____ she saw the police.

11. A police car blocked Tina _____ she tried to drive away.

12. _____ the police caught Spike and Tina, they handcuffed them and read them their rights.

**B.** Complete these sentences with the correct form of the verb.

| | | | |
|---|---|---|---|
| block | get | leave | step |
| break | grab | put | try |
| catch | handcuff | ring | |
| climb | hear | run | |
| drive | jump | see | |

1. Tina _drove_ Spike to the jewelry store.

2. Spike _____ on gloves, a mask, and a hat before he _____ out of the car.

3. Spike _____ a store window before he _____ into the store.

4. The alarm _____ as soon as Spike _____ onto the floor.

5. Spike _____ some jewelry before he _____ the store.

6. Spike _____ a police siren when he _____ out of the window.

7. The police _____ after Spike when they _____ him.

8. The police _____ Spike's foot when he _____ to climb over the wall.

9. Tina _____ to drive away when she _____ the police.

10. The police _____ Tina's car before she could drive away.

11. When they _____ Spike and Tina, they _____ them.

12. After Spike and Tina _____ into the police car, the police

_____ them to the police station.

**C.** Use the chart. Ask and answer questions about the robbery.

| Did | Spike

the police | put on gloves
break the window
take some jewelry
hear a siren
run away
chase Spike
catch Spike | before
after
when
as soon as | he got out of the car?
he climbed into the store?
he left the store?
he saw the police?
they saw him?
he climbed over a wall? |
| --- | --- | --- | --- | --- |

1. *Did Spike hear a siren when he got out of the car?*
   *No, he didn't.*

2. _____

   _____

3. _____

   _____

4. _____

   _____

5. _____

   _____

6. _____

_____

7. _____

_____

8. _____

_____

9. _____

_____

10. _____

_____

**D.** Read the story and answer the questions.

## THE BOOKING

After the police arrived at the police station with Spike and Tina, there were many procedures to complete. First, the police put Spike and Tina's names into a computer. A nationwide service called NCIC (National Crime Information Center) has computerized information on all criminals. The police wanted to find out if Spike and Tina were using their real names, and they also wanted to know if the two had been in trouble before. There was no information on Tina, but the police found out that Spike had been arrested two years ago for burglary.

Then, the police took Tina's and Spike's fingerprints. They kept one copy of prints for their own police department and sent one copy to the state and another copy to the FBI.

After the police took the prints, they took pictures of Spike and Tina for the department files. Before Spike and Tina signed the fingerprint forms, the police reread them their rights. After the police were sure the two understood their rights, they had Tina and Spike sign the forms. Their signatures were also useful as handwriting samples.

When Spike and Tina finished signing the forms, the police told them to empty their pockets and to remove their belts and shoelaces. Spike and Tina were each allowed to make one telephone call. When Spike called his lawyer, he heard his lawyer's answering machine, so the police allowed him to call his brother. Tina called her mother.

Because it was late at night and the court was closed until the next morning, Tina and Spike had to spend the night in jail.

The next morning, a judge set bail for Spike and Tina. Spike didn't use any weapons in the burglary, so the judge set his bail at $1000. Tina's bail was set at $750. Tina's mother paid her bail, and Spike's lawyer arranged to pay ten percent of his bail. They promised to appear in court in two weeks.

Answer the following questions about the story.

1. Why did the police check the NCIC?

_____

2. Was this Spike's first arrest?

_____

3. What did the police do after they checked the NCIC?

_____

4. How many copies of fingerprints did the police take?

_____

5. What did the police do before they took pictures of Spike and Tina?

_____

6. What did Spike and Tina do when they finished signing the forms?

_____

7. When did Spike call his lawyer?

_____

8. Why did the police allow Spike to make a second call?

_____

9. Why couldn't Spike and Tina go home?

_____

10. When will they appear in court?

_____

## Discussion Questions:

1. Were you ever the victim of a crime?
2. Did you ever witness a crime? Tell the class about it.

## Grammar Summary

A time clause begins with words such as **before, after, as soon as,** and **when.** A time clause has a subject and a verb. In the past tense, both the verb in the main clause and the verb in the time clause are in the past tense.

He saw the police.
He began to run.

| Main Clause | Time Clause |
|---|---|
| He began to run<br>He began to run | as soon as he saw the police.<br>when he saw the police. |

| Time Clause | Main Clause |
|---|---|
| As soon as he saw the police,*<br>When he saw the police, | he began to run.<br>he began to run. |

*__Note:__  When the time clause is first, use a comma to separate it from the main clause.

# THE ACCIDENT

## Past Continuous

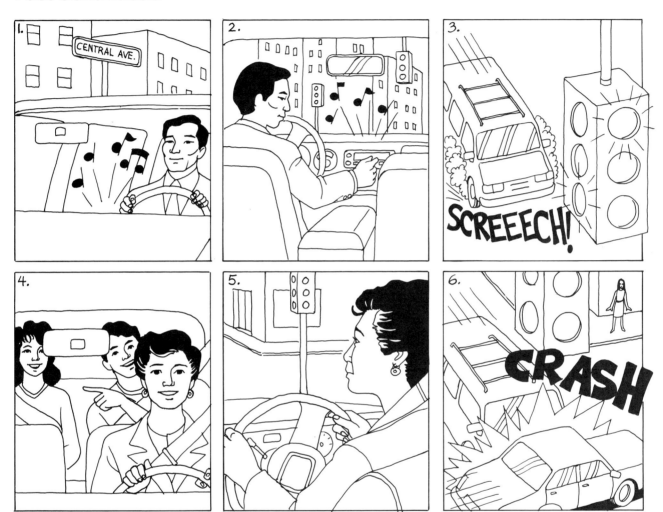

**A.** Look at the pictures and listen to your teacher describe this accident. After you listen two or three times, retell the story.

**B.** Read each sentence. Then, write the number of the matching picture on the line.

a. __2__ Lee was looking at the radio.

b. _____ Olga was driving down Main Street.

c. _____ Lee was driving home from work.

d. _____ Lee hit the side of Olga's car.

e. _____ Olga continued into the intersection.

f. _____ Her children were wearing their seatbelts.

g. _____ The light changed from yellow to red.

h. _____ Olga was driving to the store.

i. _____ No one was hurt.

j. _____ Lee decided to change the radio station.

**C.** Use the chart to form sentences about the accident.

**Example:** The children were wearing seatbelts.

| Lee<br>Olga | was<br>wasn't | driving | home.<br>to the store.<br>along Central Avenue.<br>down Main Street. |
| The children | were<br>weren't | wearing | a seatbelt.<br>seatbelts. |

**D.** Read each sentence about the accident. Circle "T" if it is true. Circle "F" if it is false.

| | | |
|---|---|---|
| 1. Lee was driving to school when the accident happened. | T | (F) |
| 2. Lee was listening to the radio while he was driving home. | T | F |
| 3. Olga was driving to the store when Lee hit her car. | T | F |
| 4. While Olga was driving, she was listening to the radio. | T | F |
| 5. When the accident happened, Lee was wearing his seatbelt. | T | F |
| 6. The children were wearing their seatbelts when the accident happened. | T | F |
| 7. Everyone was talking while they were driving to the store. | T | F |
| 8. Lee wasn't paying attention when the light changed. | T | F |
| 9. Ellen was crossing the street when the van went through the red light. | T | F |
| 10. When she saw the accident, Ellen was standing on the corner. | T | F |

**E.** Combine sentences 1 to 5 with **when.** Combine sentences 6 to 10 with **while.**

**Example 1:** Olga was wearing a seatbelt. The accident happened.
Olga was wearing a seatbelt **when** the accident happened.

**Example 2:** Olga was wearing a seatbelt. She was driving to the store.
Olga was wearing a seatbelt **while** she was driving to the store.

1. Lee wasn't wearing his seatbelt. He hit Olga's car.
2. The children were wearing seatbelts. The accident happened.
3. Olga was driving through the intersection. Lee hit her car.
4. Ellen was waiting for the green light. The accident happened.
5. Ellen was walking home from work. She saw the accident.

6. Lee was thinking about his girlfriend. He was driving home.
7. Lee was listening to the radio. He was driving.
8. Olga was driving to the store. She was talking with her children.
9. Olga was driving along Main Street. Lee was driving along Central Avenue.
10. Ellen was standing on the corner. She was waiting for the light to change.

## Writing

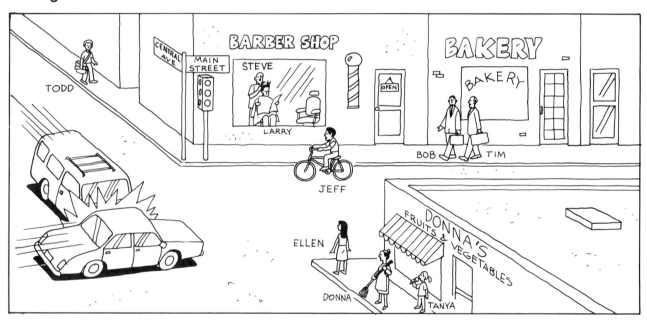

**A.** Many people saw the accident on the corner of Central Avenue and Main Street. What was each person doing when the accident happened? Use the vocabulary in the box.

| | |
|---|---|
| cut | ride |
| deliver | stand |
| eat an ice cream cone | sweep the sidewalk |
| get a haircut | talk |
| look out | walk |

1. _Donna was sweeping the sidewalk._

2. _____

3. _____

4. _____

5. _____

6. _____

7. _____

8. _____

9. _____

10. _____

**B.** Complete these sentences with the correct form of the verb.

| cut | get | read | sit | talk |
|------|--------|------|-------|------|
| deliver | happen | ride | stand | walk |
| eat | hear | see | sweep | |

1. Todd _was delivering_ newspapers when he _saw_ the accident.

2. Larry _____ in the barber shop when the accident

   _____ .

3. Larry _____ a newspaper while he _____ a haircut.

4. The barber _____ Larry's hair when he _____ the crash.

5. When Donna _____ the accident, she _____ the sidewalk.

6. While Bob and Tim _____ down the street, they _____ about business.

7. Jeff _____ his bicycle when he _____ the accident.

46

8. Bob and Tim _____ when they _____ the crash.

9. Ellen _____ on the corner when she _____ the accident.

10. While Tanya _____ down the street, she _____ an ice cream cone.

**C.** Answer these questions about the picture.

1. What was Lee doing while he was driving home?

   *He was listening to the radio.*

2. What was Todd doing when he saw the accident?

   _____

3. What was Tanya eating when she heard the crash?

   _____

4. What was Larry reading while he was sitting in the barber's chair?

   _____

5. Who was sweeping the sidewalk when the accident happened?

   _____

6. What was Jeff doing when the van hit the car?

   _____

7. What were Bob and Tim talking about while they were walking down the street?

   _____

8. Where was Ellen standing when the accident happened?

   _____

9. What was Steve doing when he heard the crash?

   _____

10. Who was riding his bicycle when Lee hit Olga's car?

    _____

**D.** Use the chart. Write five questions and answers about the accident.

| What | was | Donna<br>Larry<br>Steve<br>Todd | doing | when | the accident happened?<br>Lee went through the light?<br>Lee hit Olga's car? |
|------|-----|--------------------------------|-------|------|------------------------------------------------------------------------------|
|      | were | Bob and Tim |  |  |  |

1. *What was Larry doing when Lee went through the red light?*
*He was getting a haircut.*

2. _____

_____

3. _____

_____

4. _____

_____

5. _____

_____

**E.** Read these situations and answer the questions.

Sam was driving down the highway. His first delivery was to Ace Deli for 75 cases of soda. Suddenly, the car in front of him stopped quickly. Sam did, too. He stopped in time, but many cases of soda landed on the highway.

1. Where was Sam going?

_____

2. What was he carrying on the truck?

_____

3. Did Sam hit the car in front of him?

_____

4. Did all the soda fall off the truck?

_____

Lisa was driving past a school. It was lunchtime, and many children were playing in the schoolyard. Suddenly, a soccer ball rolled into the street. A little boy ran after it. He ran into the street in front of Lisa. She stepped on her brakes and just missed the child.

1. Why did the little boy run into the street?

_____

2. Was the little boy paying attention to the traffic?

_____

3. Did Lisa hit the boy?

_____


Darold only needed milk and bread. So, he went out to the car and put his son in the front seat next to him. He decided not to put him in the car seat because the store was only a mile away. Darold was only two blocks from his house when another car went through a stop sign. Darold slammed on his brakes, and his son hit his head on the front window.

1. Where was Darold going?

_____

2. Was his son wearing a seatbelt?

_____

3. Why didn't Darold put his son in the car seat?

_____

4. Who was hurt? Why?

_____


**Discussion Questions:**

1. Were you ever in a car accident? Did you ever witness a car accident? What happened?
2. Whose fault was the accident?
3. Was anyone hurt?
4. Did an ambulance come?
5. What were the weather conditions?
6. What was the damage to the cars?
7. Did the police come?
8. Who called the police?
9. Did the police fill out an accident report?
10. Were the cars towed away?

# Grammar Summary

**Statements:**

| I He She It | was wasn't | driving | to the store. |
|---|---|---|---|
| We You They | were weren't | | |

## When Statements:

The past continuous often occurs in time clauses with **when.** The verb in the main clause is in the past continuous. It tells about the action that started first. The verb in the **when** clause is in the simple past.

| Main Clause | When Clause |
|---|---|
| They were driving to the store Ellen was standing on the corner | when the van hit their car. when she saw the accident. |

| Time Clause | Main Clause |
|---|---|
| When the van hit their car,* When she saw the accident, | they were driving to the store. she was standing on the corner. |

**\*Note:** When the time clause is first, use a comma to separate it from the main clause.

## While Statements:

The past continuous also occurs in time clauses with **while.** It tells about two actions that were happening at the same time. The verb in both clauses is in the past continuous.

Lee **was listening** to the radio while he **was driving** home.
While Lee **was driving** home, he **was listening** to the radio.

# THE APARTMENT

## Comparative and Superlative Adjectives

**A.** Look at the pictures of two apartment buildings. Listen to your teacher, and fill in the comparative adjective. Use the adjectives from the box.

| | | |
|---|---|---|
| expensive | cheap | dangerous |
| convenient | clean | safe |
| new | high | tall |

1. Michael and Patty's building is _newer than_ Ali's building.

2. Ali's rent is _____ Michael and Patty's rent.

3. Michael and Patty's rent is _____ Ali's rent.

4. Michael and Patty's apartment is _____ Ali's.

5. Ali's neighborhood is _____ Michael and Patty's.

6. Ali's building is _____ Michael and Patty's.

7. Michael and Patty's neighborhood is _____ Ali's neighborhood.

8. Michael and Patty's neighborhood is _____ Ali's neighborhood.

9. Michael and Patty's building is _____ Ali's building.

10. Michael and Patty's neighborhood is _____ Ali's neighborhood.

**B.** Read two facts about the apartments. Make a sentence using the comparative adjective in parentheses.

1. Michael and Patty's building is five years old. Ali's building is sixty-three years old.   (new)

2. Michael and Patty's apartment has four rooms. Ali's apartment has two rooms.   (big)

3. There are many stores near Ali's building. There are only two stores near Michael and Patty's apartment.   (convenient)

4. Ali's building is four stories high. Michael and Patty's building is fifteen stories high.   (small)

5. Michael and Patty's neighborhood has clean streets and many trees. Ali's neighborhood has dirty streets and few trees.   (attractive)

6. Ali's rent is $350 a month. Michael and Patty's rent is $800 a month.   (cheap)

7. There are many crimes in Ali's neighborhood. There are few crimes in Michael and Patty's neighborhood.   (dangerous)

8. Michael and Patty's building has a doorman and a video screen. Ali's building has an intercom.   (safe)

9. Michael and Patty's building is thirty minutes from their jobs. Ali's building is only ten minutes from his job.   (convenient)

10. There is a lot of garbage and litter near Ali's building. There is almost no litter or garbage near Michael and Patty's building.   (dirty)

**C.** Use the chart. Form sentences about the apartments.

| | | | | |
|---|---|---|---|---|
| Ali's apartment<br><br>Michael and Patty's apartment | is | older<br>cheaper<br>safer<br>smaller | than | Michael and Patty's apartment.<br><br>Ali's apartment. |
| | | more<br>less | convenient<br>comfortable<br>expensive<br>dangerous | |

**D.** Look at the chart describing the three apartments. Read each sentence. Circle "T" if it is true. Circle "F" if it is false.

| | Michael & Patty's | Ali's | Ann's |
|---|---|---|---|
| **Age of building** | 5 years old | 63 years old | 20 years old |
| **Rent** | $800/month | $350/month | $650/month |
| **Number of floors** | 15 | 4 | 10 |
| **Number of rooms** | 4 | 2 | 3 |
| **Convenience** | not convenient | very convenient | convenient |
| **Neighborhood** | safe | dangerous | very safe |
| **Neighbors** | not friendly | very friendly | friendly |
| **Superintendent** | helpful | not helpful | very helpful |

1. Ali's building is the oldest.      (T)   F
2. Ann's apartment is the cheapest.      T   F
3. Michael and Patty's building is the tallest.      T   F
4. Ann's apartment is the most convenient.      T   F
5. Ali's building is the safest.      T   F
6. Michael and Patty's neighbors are the friendliest.      T   F
7. Ali's apartment is the most expensive.      T   F
8. Ali's neighborhood is the most dangerous.      T   F
9. Michael and Patty's superintendent is the most helpful.      T   F
10. Ali's superintendent is the least helpful.      T   F

**E.** Answer these **Which** or **Whose** questions about the apartments.

**Example 1:** Which building is the tallest?
**Ali's is.**

**Example 2:** Whose apartment is more expensive, Ann's or Ali's?
**Ann's is.**

1. Which building is the oldest?
2. Which apartment is the least expensive?
3. Which apartment is the smallest?
4. Which building is the most convenient?
5. Which neighborhood is the most dangerous?
6. Which superintendent is the least helpful?
7. Whose apartment is cheaper, Ali's or Ann's?
8. Whose building is taller, Ann's or Michael and Patty's?
9. Whose neighborhood is safer, Michael and Patty's or Ali's?
10. Whose neighbors are friendlier, Michael and Patty's or Ann's?
11. Whose superintendent is the most helpful?
12. Whose neighbors are the friendliest?

## WRITING

**A.** Circle the correct adjective form.

1. Michael and Patty's apartment is **more expensive than** / **the most expensive.**
2. Ali's building is **older than** / **the oldest.**
3. Ann's apartment is **bigger than** / **the biggest** Ali's apartment.
4. Ali's apartment is **smaller than** / **the smallest** Ann's apartment.
5. Michael and Patty's neighborhood is **safer than** / **the safest** Ali's neighborhood.
6. Ann's neighborhood is **safer than** / **the safest.**
7. Ali's neighborhood is **more dangerous than** / **the most dangerous** Michael and Patty's.
8. Ali's neighbors are **friendlier than** / **the friendliest** Ann's neighbors.
9. Michael and Patty's neighbors are **less friendly than** / **the least friendly.**
10. Ann's superintendent is **more helpful than** / **the most helpful.**

**B.** Read these facts about the apartments. Write a comparative or superlative sentence.

1. Ali's apartment is sixty-three years old. Ann's apartment is twenty years old.

   *Ali's apartment is older than Ann's.*

2. Ali's rent is $350 a month, Ann's rent is $650 a month, and Michael and Patty's rent is $800 a month.

   _____

3. Ann's building is ten stories high. Michael and Patty's building is fifteen stories high.

   _____

4. Ali's apartment has two rooms, Ann's apartment has three rooms, and Michael and Patty's apartment has four rooms.

   _____

5. Michael and Patty's building is twenty minutes from a grocery store. Ali's building is five minutes from a grocery store. Ann's building is ten minutes from a grocery store.

   _____

6. There is a lot of crime in Ali's neighborhood. There is almost no crime in Ann's neighborhood.

   _____

7. Ann's neighbors sometimes speak to each other. Ali's neighbors always speak to each other.

   _____

8. Michael and Patty's neighbors never speak to each other. Ann's neighbors sometimes speak to each other. Ali's neighbors always speak to each other.

   _____

9. Ali's superintendent rarely fixes anything in the building. Ann's superintendent sometimes fixes everything right away.

   _____

10. Ali's superintendent rarely fixes anything in the building. Ann's superintendent sometimes fixes things. Michael and Patty's superintendent fixes everything right away.

    _____

**C.** Fill in the information about **your** apartment or house.

| | Ann's | Ali's | My apt./house |
|---|---|---|---|
| **Rent/mortgage** | $650/month | $350/month | |
| **Number of rooms** | 3 | 2 | |
| **Number of floors** | 10 | 4 | |
| **Neighborhood** | very safe | dangerous | |
| **Convenience** | convenient | very convenient | |
| **Minutes to school** | 30 minutes | 10 minutes | |
| **Neighbors** | friendly | very friendly | |

Then, complete these sentences using the chart and the adjectives in parentheses.

1. My rent is _____ Ann's.   (expensive)

2. My apartment/house is _____ Ali's.   (small/big)

3. My neighborhood is _____ Ali's.   (safe/dangerous)

4. My apartment/house is _____ Ann's.   (convenient)

5. My apartment/house is _____ Ali's.   (convenient)

6. My neighbors are _____ Ali's.   (friendly)

Write four sentences comparing your apartment/house to Ann's and Ali's.

7. _____

8. _____

9. _____

10. _____

**D.** Read the story. Then, write nine sentences comparing the houses.

## HOUSE-HUNTING

Susan and Paul are expecting a baby soon. Right now they're living in a one-bedroom apartment. They've decided to move into a house so that they'll have more room. They think a one-bedroom apartment will be too small for them after the baby is born. Paul's mother is a real estate agent, so she's helping them find a house. So far, they've seen three houses, but they can't decide which one to buy.

First, Susan and Paul looked at a twelve-year-old ranch-style house on Smith Street. It is only twenty minutes from their offices. It has two bedrooms, a living room, a dining room, a kitchen, a bathroom, and a large unfinished basement. Susan likes it because it has a fireplace and a large backyard. Paul isn't sure about it. It doesn't have much closet space, and he would like to have a third bedroom to use as an office. The house is in a nice neighborhood, but the schools aren't very good. It has a detached one-car garage, but it has a long driveway, so they could park the second car in the driveway. The asking price is $110,000.

Next, they looked at a small ten-year-old two-story house on Hope Street. That house is ten minutes from their offices. It also has two bedrooms, a living room, and a dining room, and it has a large kitchen. There is a lot of closet space. There is one full bathroom upstairs and a powder room on the first floor. It has a basement, but it will need a lot of work before it is usable. The backyard is very small, so Susan won't be able to put in a pool. Paul likes the house because the garage is attached. Paul won't have to worry about mowing a big lawn because it doesn't have a front lawn. The neighborhood is okay on that block, but three blocks away there is a lot of crime. The asking price is $70,000.

Finally, Paul's mother showed them a beautiful Victorian house on Brook Street. It is 80 years old. The house is forty-five minutes from their offices in a very nice neighborhood. The house needs painting, new plumbing, and a new roof, but it has three bedrooms, a living room with a fireplace, a dining room, a very large kitchen with a pantry, and it has a deck. There are two and a half bathrooms and a lot of closet space. The backyard is big enough for a pool, and there is also a large front lawn. There is a two-car garage in the back. There are many excellent schools in the area. The asking price is $170,000. Both Susan and Paul love the house, but they think it is too expensive for them.

Write nine sentences comparing these houses.

1. _____

2. _____

3. _____

4. _____

5. _____

6. _____

7. _____

8. _____

9. _____

10. Which house do you think they should buy?

_____

## Discussion Questions:

1. Do you live in an apartment or a house? Describe it.
2. What do you like about it? What don't you like about it?
3. Do you like your neighborhood? Explain why or why not.
4. How does your home in the U.S. compare with your home in your native country?
5. Do you want to move? Why or why not?

## Comparative Adjectives:

When you compare two things, use the comparative form of the adjective.

Ali's apartment is **older than** Ann's apartment.
Ali's apartment is **more convenient than** Ann's apartment.

| Ali's apartment | is | _____ er  <br> more _____ | than | Ann's apartment. |
|---|---|---|---|---|

## Superlative Adjectives:

When you compare three or more things, use the superlative form of the adjective.

| Ali's apartment | is | the | _____ est.  <br> most _____ . |
|---|---|---|---|

58

# RETIREMENT PLANS

**May, Might, Maybe, Perhaps**

**A.** Jack is going to retire next month. He is thinking about things he might do. Read each sentence. Then, write the number of the matching picture on the line.

a. _____ He might join a health club.

b. _____ He might buy a bicycle.

c. _____ He might travel.

d. _____ He may get a part-time job.

e. _____ He may visit his sister in Arizona.

f. _____ Maybe he will get a dog.

g. _____ Maybe he will plant a vegetable garden.

h. _____ Maybe he will volunteer at the library.

i. _____ Perhaps he will sell his house.

j. _____ Perhaps he will learn how to use a computer.

**B.** Use the chart to form sentences about Jack.

**Example:** Jack may join a health club.

| | | | |
|---|---|---|---|
| Jack | might<br><br>may | buy<br>move<br>get<br>join<br>visit | a mobile home.<br>a bicycle.<br>to California.<br>to an apartment.<br>a dog.<br>a part-time job.<br>a health club.<br>his daughter.<br>his sister in Arizona. |

**C.** Ask and answer questions about Jack's retirement plans.

| I'm not sure. | Perhaps he will.<br>Maybe he will.<br>He might.<br>He may. |
|---|---|
| I don't think so. | |

**Example:** start a business?
Will Jack start a business?
I'm not sure. Perhaps he will.

1. buy a computer?
2. take a course at the community college?
3. paint his house?
4. get a cat?
5. travel around the world?
6. buy a sports car?
7. get married?
8. spend time at the senior citizens' center?
9. move to an apartment?
10. plant a flower garden?

**D.** Complete these sentences about Jack's retirement plans.

**Example 1:** Jack likes animals, so…
Jack likes animals, so he might get a cat.
**Example 2:** Jack's son has a small business, so…
Jack's son has a small business, so perhaps Jack will work for him part-time.

1. Jack loves the climate in California, so…
2. Jack's house is too big, so…
3. Jack has never been to Europe, so…
4. Jack needs to exercise more, so…
5. Jack is lonely, so…
6. Jack loves the country and he loves to fish, so…
7. Jack is very interested in computers, so…
8. Jack loves to eat fresh vegetables, so…
9. Jack likes to read and spend time in the library, so…
10. Jack's daughter lives in Florida, so…

## Writing

**A.** Complete these sentences with **perhaps** or **maybe** and the correct form of the verb.

| Perhaps<br>Maybe | buy | move | take |
| | get | plant | travel |
| | join | start | visit |

1. *Perhaps* Jack *will join* a health club.

2. _____ he _____ his daughter in Florida.

3. _____ he _____ a bicycle.

4. _____ he _____ a small business.

5. _____ he _____ around Europe.

6. _____ he _____ married.

7. _____ he _____ to an apartment.

8. _____ he _____ a flower garden.

9. _____ he _____ a course at the community college.

10. _____ he _____ a dog.

**B.** Answer these questions about Jack with **may** or **might.** Give two choices in your answer.

1. Where will Jack travel? (Italy, Spain)

   *He may visit Italy, or he may visit Spain.*

2. If Jack sells his house, where will he live? (apartment, condo)

   *He might rent an apartment, or he might buy a condo.*

3. What kind of vegetables will Jack plant? (carrots, beans)

   _____

4. Whom will Jack visit? (sister, daughter)

   _____

5. What will Jack do for exercise? (swim, jog)

   _____

6. Where will Jack go on vacation? (Mexico, Puerto Rico)

_____

7. Where will Jack volunteer? (library, hospital)

_____

8. Where will Jack move? (California, Florida)

_____

9. What kind of pet will Jack get? (dog, cat)

_____

10. Where will Jack work? (bakery, hardware store)

_____

11. What will Jack do with his house? (sell it, keep it)

_____

12. What course will Jack take at college? (art, computers)

_____

C. Read the story, and then answer the questions.

Jack lives in New Jersey. He owns a three-bedroom house with a large yard. Jack is 65, and every year the house and yard seem bigger and bigger. It takes a long time to cut the grass and take care of the yard. Jack is thinking about moving. He might stay in New Jersey and move to an apartment. His brothers and his son live in New Jersey, and all his friends are there.

But Jack might move to South Florida. In Florida, the skies are blue and the temperature is usually above 75°. His daughter, son-in-law, and their three children live only a few miles from the Gulf of Mexico. But he's worried about living with his daughter. Perhaps the children will be too noisy. His daughter is thinking about returning to work, so she might want him to baby-sit all the time.

Jack's sister lives in Arizona. Jack loves the climate and the countryside there. But, his sister may drive him crazy because she talks all the time.

Jack isn't sure what he will do.

1. Does Jack live by himself?

_____

2. Why is Jack thinking about moving?

_____

3. Why does he like living in New Jersey?

_____

4. What does Jack like about Florida?

_____

5. Does Jack want to baby-sit for his grandchildren?

_____

6. Is Jack going to move to Arizona?

_____

7. Why is Jack worried about living with his sister?

_____

8. Where is Jack going to move?

_____


**D.** Read these situations and answer the questions.

Jack wants to travel around the United States. A friend is selling his mobile home. It's just the right size for one or two people.

1. Will Jack travel around the United States?

_____

2. What will he buy?

_____

3. Will he travel alone or with a friend?

_____

Jack's wife died ten years ago. He's dating a kind, loving woman. He loves her, but he doesn't know if he wants to marry her.

1. Did Jack remarry after his wife died?

_____

2. How does he feel about this woman?

_____

3. Will he marry her?

_____

There are several retirement communities near Jack. The houses are small, with one or two bedrooms. For a monthly maintenance fee, the management of the communities takes care of the exterior of the houses.

1. Are the homes in these communities larger or smaller than Jack's?

_____

2. Who paints the houses?

_____

3. Will Jack move to a retirement community?

_____

## Discussion Questions:

1. What is the retirement age in the United States?
2. Is there a retirement age in your country?
3. Does your company have a retirement plan?
4. Where do people live after they retire (e.g., a retirement community, senior citizen housing)?
5. Why do some retirees move to a different area?
6. How old are your parents or grandparents? Are they retired?
7. Where do they live?
8. Whom do they live with?
9. If they are retired, what interests or hobbies do they have?

# Grammar Summary

**May, might, maybe,** and **perhaps** express possibility.

## May and might:

| | may | | a computer. |
|---|---|---|---|
| Jack | | buy | |
| | might | | a bicycle. |

## Perhaps and maybe:

| Perhaps | | | | a computer. |
|---|---|---|---|---|
| | Jack | will | buy | |
| Maybe | | | | a bicycle. |

## Must / Have to

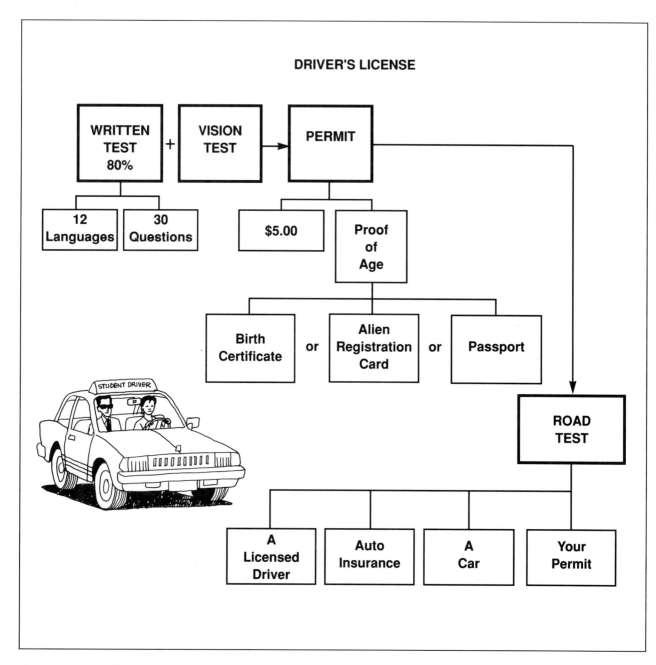

**DRIVER'S LICENSE**

WRITTEN TEST 80% + VISION TEST → PERMIT

WRITTEN TEST 80%:
- 12 Languages
- 30 Questions

PERMIT:
- $5.00
- Proof of Age
  - Birth Certificate or Alien Registration Card or Passport

STUDENT DRIVER

ROAD TEST:
- A Licensed Driver
- Auto Insurance
- A Car
- Your Permit

**A.** Teresa needs a car to get to her part-time job, but she needs to get a driver's license. Look at the chart and listen to your teacher talk about the many things Teresa must do in order to get a license. After you listen two or three times, retell the information.

**B.** Read each sentence about the chart. Circle "T" if it is true. Circle "F" if it is false.

| | | |
|---|---|---|
| 1. Teresa must take two tests to get her permit. | Ⓣ | F |
| 2. Teresa has to take the test in English. | T | F |
| 3. Teresa must get 90% on the written test. | T | F |
| 4. Teresa must get a permit before she takes the road test. | T | F |
| 5. She must pay for her permit. | T | F |
| 6. Teresa has to show proof of age. | T | F |
| 7. Teresa must show her birth certificate for proof of age. | T | F |
| 8. She must buy a new car to get a license. | T | F |
| 9. Teresa has to have a job to get a license. | T | F |
| 10. She must go to the road test with a licensed driver. | T | F |

**C.** Use the chart. Make sentences about the chart.

**Example:** Teresa has to pass a written test in order to get her permit.

| Teresa | must<br><br>has to | get<br>have<br>pass<br>pay<br>show | proof of age<br>a permit<br>five dollars<br>80% on the written test<br>a written test<br>a vision test<br>a car<br>a road test<br>a car with insurance | in order to get a permit.<br><br><br>in order to take the road test.<br><br><br>in order to get a license. |
|---|---|---|---|---|

**D.** Say each sentence again. Use **must not.**

**Example:** <u>Don't go</u> through a red light!
   <u>You must not</u> go through a red light.

1. Don't pass cars on the right.
2. Don't drive recklessly.
3. Don't drink and drive.
4. Don't drive over the speed limit.
5. Don't drive over 25 mph in a school zone.
6. Don't leave the scene of an accident.
7. Don't drive without wearing your seatbelt.
8. Don't pass through a stop sign.
9. Don't drive too closely to the driver in front of you.
10. Don't drive without a license.

**E.** Say each sentence again. Use **doesn't have to.**

**Example:** It's not necessary for Teresa to get 100% on the written test.
Teresa doesn't have to get 100% on the written test.

1. It's not necessary for Teresa to take the test in English.
2. It's not necessary for Teresa to be an American citizen.
3. It's not necessary for Teresa to own a car.
4. It's not necessary for her to be 21 to get a license.
5. It's not necessary for her to have perfect vision.
6. It's not necessary for her to pay $20.00 for her permit.
7. It's not necessary for Teresa to show her birth certificate.
8. It's not necessary for Teresa to go to private driving school.
9. It's not necessary for Teresa to make an appointment to take the written test.
10. It's not necessary for Teresa to speak English.

## WRITING

**A.** Fill in the blanks with the correct modal.

| | | |
|---|---|---|
| must | has to | doesn't have to |
| must not | have to | don't have to |

1. You _don't have to_ take the written test in English.

2. You _____ drive over the speed limit.

3. You _____ pay five dollars when you get your permit.

4. You _____ stop at a red light.

5. All drivers _____ drive carefully.

6. Children under five _____ ride in car seats.

7. Teresa _____ have seatbelts in the front seat of her car.

8. You _____ have a radio in your car.

9. Drivers _____ take their cars to the inspection station once a year.

10. Teresa _____ drive on the wrong side of the street.

11. Teresa _____ take a vision test.

12. You _____ wash your car regularly.

13. Children _____ ride in cars without wearing seatbelts.

14. If you fail the written test, you _____ wait seven days before taking the test again.

15. You _____ be 17 to drive a vehicle that is only for farm use.

**B.** Write each sentence again. Use **has to, doesn't have to, must, or must not.**

1. It is necessary for Teresa to pay all her traffic fines.

   *Teresa has to pay all her traffic fines.*

2. It is against the law for you to drive without a license.

   *You must not drive without a license.*

3. It is not necessary for Teresa to renew her license in person.

   _____

4. It is necessary for you to carry your license with you when you drive.

   _____

5. It is against the law for you to leave the scene of an accident.

   _____

6. It is against the law to drink any alcoholic beverage while driving.

   _____

7. It is necessary for you to get a permit before you get a driver's license.

   _____

8. It is necessary for Teresa to have auto insurance.

   _____

9. It is against the law to drive on a sidewalk.

   _____

10. It is necessary for Teresa to pass the road test to get a license.

   _____

**C.** Read the story. Then, answer the questions.

Thirty minutes ago, Tom, 17, and his girlfriend, Denise, 16, were at a graduation party at their friend Jimmy's house. Jimmy's parents weren't home, and soon most of the people at the party were drinking even though most of them were under 21. Tom drank some beer, but Denise only drank soda. She had to be home by 1:00, so she asked Tom to take her home.

When they got in the car, Denise was worried. Tom looked a little drunk, but he said he was okay. He knew he had to be careful because the police often set up roadblocks on graduation night to check for drunk drivers.

As they were driving down the highway, a police car signaled Tom to pull over. Tom had to show an officer his license and to get out of the car. He had to prove he was sober, but it was very difficult because he drank three cans of beer at the party. He had to walk a straight line, take a breath test, and answer some questions. The police determined that he was too drunk to drive, so they arrested him. They took Tom and Denise to the police station. Both Tom and Denise were very upset. After they arrived at the police station, Tom and Denise had to call their parents. Because they were minors, their parents had to come to the station to pick them up. Tom wasn't in an accident, so the police sergeant didn't make him stay in jail overnight.

This was Tom's first offense, so he didn't have to give up his license; instead, the judge put him on probation for six months. He had to pay a $300 fine. He also had to spend thirty days at a local boys' club as a youth volunteer. Denise didn't have to pay a fine because she wasn't drunk and she wasn't driving the car, but her parents said she was grounded for one month.

1. Why were Tom and Denise at Jimmy's house?

   _____

2. Why did Tom and Denise leave the party?

   _____

3. How did Tom know about the police roadblocks?

   _____

4. Why did the police set up roadblocks on graduation night?

   _____

5. What did Tom have to do to prove that he was sober?

   _____

6. Did Tom pass the tests?  How do you know?

   _____

7. Why did Tom's parents have to go to the police station?

   _____

8. Did Tom have to spend the night in jail?

_____

9. What was Tom's punishment?

_____

10. What was Denise's punishment?

_____

11. What does *grounded* mean?

_____

12. Why do you think Denise's parents punished her?

_____

**D.** Read each cartoon. Fill in the conversation between the driver and the police officer. Use one of the expressions in the box for the driver's part of the conversation. Then, write the traffic rule. Use **must** or **must not**.

| | |
|---|---|
| What's the matter? | What's the trouble? |
| What's the problem? | What did I do? |

**Example:**

Driver: What's the problem?

Officer: You were driving with a broken headlight.

Rule: *You must not drive with a broken headlight.*

1.

Officer: You didn't pull over for the ambulance.

Rule: _____

2.

Officer: Why are you driving on the sidewalk?

Rule: _____

71

3.

You went through a red light.

Rule: _____

4.

You were tailgating.

Rule: _____

5.

You're not wearing a helmet.

Rule: _____

6.

You can't make a U turn here.

Rule: _____

7.

You were speeding!

Rule: _____

8.

I saw you drinking beer.

Rule: _____

# Grammar Summary

**Have to** and **must** express obligation or necessity.

| I | have to / must | pay | for a license. |
|---|---|---|---|
| She | has to / must | | the fine. |

**Don't have to** expresses that an action is not necessary.

| I | don't have to | wash the car. |
|---|---|---|
| She | doesn't have to | |

**Must not** expresses that an action is unlawful or not permitted.

| I / She | must not | drive without a license. |
|---|---|---|

# UNIT 11
# COLLEGE LIFE

## Present Perfect with For and Since

GINA    one year

JOE    two years

MELISSA    three years

**A.** Listen to your teacher talk about three students at Kentucky State College. After you listen two or three times, retell the information.

**B.** Read each sentence. Which student does it describe: Gina, Joe, or Melissa?

Example:    This student hasn't studied very hard. That's Joe.

1. This student has been at school for a year.
2. This student has worked at the school library.
3. This student has written a lot of letters to her boyfriend.
4. These students have lived in the dorm since they started college.
5. This student lives in an apartment off campus.

6. This student has failed a lot of tests since September.

7. This student has been at college for three years.

8. This student has worked at the college radio station for two years.

9. This student has cleaned a lot of tables since September.

10. This student has studied engineering since the fall.

**C.** Use the chart. Form sentences about the students.

**Example:** Melissa has worked at the library since she started college.

| Gina<br><br>Joe<br><br>Melissa | has<br><br>hasn't | been<br>worked<br>studied<br>lived | in college<br>at the cafeteria<br>at the library<br>at the radio station | for | one year.<br>two years.<br>three years. |
| | | | engineering<br>theology<br>business<br>in the dorm<br>in an apartment | since | 19__.<br>September.<br>he/she began college. |

**D.** College life is very different from life at home. Talk about the things these students haven't done since September.

**Examples:** They used to see their high school friends all the time.
They haven't seen their high school friends since September.

1. They used to see their families everyday.

2. They used to sleep in comfortable beds.

3. Gina used to go out with her boyfriend every weekend.

4. Gina used to drive her mother's car.

5. Melissa used to go to bed early.

6. She used to have her own telephone.

7. Joe used to get good grades.

8. Joe used to walk his dog everyday.

9. These students used to eat home-cooked meals.

10. They used to have a lot of free time.

**E.** Answer these questions about the students and yourself.

| Yes, s/he has. | Yes, I have. | Yes, they have. |
| No, s/he hasn't. | No, I haven't. | No, they haven't. |

1. Has Gina studied engineering for a year?
2. Have these students been at college since September?
3. Have you been at college since September?
4. Has Melissa worked at the college bookstore for two years?
5. Has Joe lived in an apartment for two years?
6. Have Melissa and Gina shared an apartment for a year?
7. Have these students attended their classes?
8. Have you attended all of your classes since you started school?
9. Has Joe failed a lot of tests since September?
10. Have you passed all your tests since September?

## Writing

**A.** Circle the correct answer, **for** or **since.**

**For** tells an amount of time, e.g., the number of days, months, or years.
**Since** tells when an action started.

| for | one year<br>two years<br>a semester | since | September<br>199_<br>s/he started college |

1. Gina has been in college  **for** / **(since)** September.
2. Joe has been in college  **for** / **since**  199_.
3. Melissa has been in college  **for** / **since**  three years.
4. Those students have been in college  **for** / **since**  a long time.
5. Melissa has worked at the library  **for** / **since**  199_.
6. Melissa has read a lot of books  **for** / **since**  she started college.
7. Joe has worked at the radio station  **for** / **since**  two years.
8. He has played a lot of songs  **for** / **since**  the fall.
9. Gina has worked at the cafeteria  **for** / **since**  nine months.
10. Gina has made a lot of hamburgers  **for** / **since**  her first day of work.

**B.** Complete these sentences with the correct form of the verb. Some are negative.

| be | live | spend |
|----|------|-------|
| call | see | volunteer |
| have | study | write |

1. Gina *hasn't seen* her boyfriend since September.

2. She _____ him a lot of letters.

3. He _____ her every weekend.

4. Joe _____ in college for two years.

5. Joe _____ hard since September.

6. He _____ a lot of time at the radio station.

7. He _____ several jobs as a disc jockey at school parties.

8. Melissa _____ in the college dorm since she began college.

9. She _____ at the homeless shelter for three years.

10. She _____ theology since her sophomore year.

**C.** These students have studied and worked hard since they started school. Use these pictures to write about their activities. Use **a lot of** in every sentence.

*They have made a lot of friends since they started college.*

1. make / friends  started college

_____

_____

2. wash / dishes  September

3. play / records     the fall

4. write / letters     she left home

5. read / books     the first day of school

6. write / papers     classes began

7. volunteer / time at the shelter     September

_____

_____

8. attend / football games    the fall

_____

_____

9. make / hamburgers    she began to work

_____

_____

10. type / papers    the first day of class

**D.** Read the story. Then, answer the questions.

"Is all the equipment in the van?" Joe asks.

"Almost. The stereo, turntable, and speakers are all in. I just have to get the last box of records," responds Ernie.

Ernie runs into the house, and Joe gets behind the wheel. It is 7:00 Saturday night. It's raining. Ernie loads the last box of records, locks the van doors, and tells Joe, "I'll see you at the college." Joe starts driving. In a half hour he will be setting up his equipment at the college. Tonight he is the DJ for the college holiday party. He has studied business at the college for two years, but on weekends he earns his money as a DJ. He loves his job. He loves to watch people enjoy themselves. He loves the music. He has been a volunteer at the college radio station for two years. He was a station technician last year, but now he has his own show. He's happy and proud of himself, but his father is upset. His father has always wanted him to go into the family business. Joe has never wanted any part of the business. His father has complained since last semester, "Your grades have been going down. You haven't done your homework. You've failed several tests this month." Joe doesn't want to upset his father, but …

The rain has stopped. Joe pulls into the parking lot in front of the gym. He starts to unload the records. He's looking forward to working here tonight. He's happy. This is a good experience and might lead to his becoming a professional one day. He has decided to listen to his heart, not his father.

1. The equipment is in the van. Where are the records?

   _____.

2. Where is Joe?

   _____.

3. What time will Joe arrive at the college?

   _____.

4. Why is Joe going to the college tonight?

   _____.

5. Has he gotten paid to work at the college radio station?

   _____.

6. How is Joe doing in school?

   _____.

7. Why isn't his father happy?

   _____.

8. Has the weather changed by the time Joe arrives?

   _____.

9. What's Joe's goal?

   _____.

10. Will he go into the family business?

   _____.

# Grammar Summary

The **present perfect** tense talks about an action that started in the past and continues into the present. The action is not complete.

**Statement:**

| I You We They | have haven't | been | at college | for | one year. two years. |
|---|---|---|---|---|---|
| He She It | has hasn't | lived | in the dorm | since | 199_. September. |

**Yes/No Questions:**

| Have | I you we they | been | at college | for | one year? two years? |
|---|---|---|---|---|---|
| Has | he she it | lived | in the dorm | since | 199_? September? |

# THE JOB INTERVIEW

## Present Perfect with Ever

---

═══════ RÉSUMÉ ═══════

### Robert Elder
### 15 County Line Road
### Madison, Florida

**Employment**

| | |
|---|---|
| 1985–present | **Union Tool**<br>Accounts Receivable Clerk |
| 1980–1984 | **Union Tool**<br>Office Clerk |

**Education**

| | |
|---|---|
| 1985–1990 | **Florida State University**<br>B.A. |
| 1980–1984 | **Madison County College**<br>A.A. |

---

**A.** This chart shows Robert's education and work experience from 1980 to the present. Read each statement. Circle "P" for past, "PP" for present perfect.

1. Robert received his A.A. from Madison County College.    (P)    PP
2. He has always worked in an accounting department.    P    PP
3. He has been at Union Tool for many years.    P    PP
4. He graduated from Florida State in 1990.    P    PP
5. Robert was a clerk from 1980 to 1984.    P    PP
6. He has never had a serious problem at work.    P    PP

|   |   |   |   |
|---|---|---|---|
| 7. He has had a lot of experience in accounting. | P | PP |
| 8. Robert went to school part-time while he worked full time. | P | PP |
| 9. Robert has received two promotions. | P | PP |
| 10. Robert received a promotion in 1985. | P | PP |
| 11. He finished his B.A. in 1990. | P | PP |
| 12. Robert has decided to look for a job in a larger company. | P | PP |

**B.** Talk about Robert's work experience at Union Tool. Use the words in bold print.

**Example 1:** Robert always (**be**) an excellent employee.
Robert **has always been** an excellent employee.

**Example 2:** Robert (**attend**) business meetings from time to time.
Robert **has attended** business meetings from time to time.

1. He always (**arrive**) on time.
2. He never (**miss**) work without notice.
3. He never (**have**) a problem with his boss.
4. Robert always (**be**) polite to customers.
5. He never (**receive**) a warning notice.
6. He (**make**) an accounting error from time to time.
7. He (**train**) new employees several times.
8. He (**manage**) the office a few times.
9. He (**learn**) new computer programs several times.
10. He (**supervise**) other workers a few times.

**C.** Use the chart. Form sentences about Robert's work experience. Tell about your work experience, too.

**Examples:** Robert has never missed work without notice.
I have had a problem with a co-worker a few times.

| | | | | |
|---|---|---|---|---|
| Robert | has | (always) | been late<br>missed work without notice<br>worked overtime<br>had a problem with the boss | |
| | | | had a problem with a co-worker<br>attended business meetings | (several times).<br>(a few times).<br>(from time to time). |
| I | have | (never) | used a computer<br>made a serious mistake | |

**D.** This chart lists Robert's work responsibilities at Union Tool. Answer these questions about Robert's work experience.

| Office Clerk | Accounts Payable Clerk |
|---|---|
| operate switchboard | handle customer complaints |
| take telephone orders | post checks |
| enter orders into a computer | make collection calls |
| prepare deposit slips | monitor accounts receivable |
| make bank deposits | produce invoices |
| file accounts | check credit references |
| process sales returns | prepare monthly statements |

Yes, he has.
No, he hasn't.

**Example:** Has Robert ever operated a switchboard?     **Yes, he has.**

1. Has he ever taken telephone orders?
2. Has he ever used a computer?
3. Has he ever monitored accounts receivable?
4. Has he ever managed the company?
5. Has he ever filled out corporate tax returns?
6. Has he ever handled customer complaints?
7. Has he ever prepared monthly statements?
8. Has he ever made collection calls?
9. Has he ever written an annual report?
10. Has he ever checked credit references?


**E.** Complete these sentences.

but he's willing to learn.

**Example:** He's never used that computer system, but he'd like to try.

but he's confident he could.

1. I've never worked in an accounting office, but…
2. He's never written an annual report, but…
3. I've never managed the office, but…
4. He's never handled the general ledger, but…
5. I've never taken a management course, but…
6. He's never filed a corporate tax return, but…
7. He's never interviewed new employees, but…
8. I've never set up new office procedures, but…
9. I've never operated a switchboard, but…
10. He's never written evaluations of other employees, but…

## Writing

**A.** Complete these sentences with the present perfect tense.

| | | |
|---|---|---|
| apply | have | receive |
| be | make | use |
| decide | manage | want |

1. Robert _has_ never _had_ a problem with a co-worker.

2. He _____ several promotions at work.

3. He _____ the office when the accounts receivable clerk has been sick.

4. He _____ a few errors, but none of them _____ serious.

5. Robert _____ always _____ cooperative and professional with the customers.

6. His boss _____ never _____ a complaint about his performance.

7. Robert _____ never _____ that computer system, but he's willing to learn.

8. Robert _____ to look for another job.

9. Robert _____ for a job at a large company.

10. He _____ always _____ to manage an accounting department.

**B.** Some of these sentences are past, others are present perfect. Circle the correct form of the verb.

1. Robert **trained** / **has trained** new employees from time to time.
2. Robert **trained** / **has trained** a new office clerk last month.
3. Robert **worked** / **has worked** as an office clerk from 1980 to 1984.
4. He **worked** / **has worked** as an accounts payable clerk for a long time.
5. Robert **missed** / **has missed** a week of work when he had the flu last year.
6. Robert **missed** / **has missed** only a few days of work at Union Tool.
7. Robert **used** / **has used** a computer in all of his work at Union Tool.
8. Robert first **used** / **has used** a computer when he was an office clerk.
9. Robert **attended** / **has attended** a business meeting last month.
10. Robert **attended** / **has attended** several important business meetings in the last three years.

**C.** Write a question for each answer. Use **ever** in each question.

1. *Has Robert ever worked for a large company?*

   No, he has never worked for a large company.

2. *Have you ever had an interview?*

   No, I have never had an interview.

3. _____

   No, I have never taken an accounting course.

4. _____

   Yes, he has produced invoices many times.

5. _____

   Yes, he has often handled complaints on the phone.

6. _____

   Yes, I have often taken telephone orders.

7. _____

   Yes, he has used this computer system a few times.

8. _____

   No, I have never worked for that company.

9. _____

   No, he has never written an annual report.

10. _____

   Yes, I have written memos in English several times.

**D.** Read this story. Then, answer these questions.

Robert has just walked into the personnel office at National Machines. He's applying for a position in their accounting department, and he really wants this job. He has never had an interview for such a good job, and he is very nervous. His heart is beating quickly, and his palms are beginning to sweat. It is one of the most stressful experiences he has ever had. He has always wanted to work for this company because they offer many opportunities for advancement, good salaries and benefits, and it is located near his home. The job is interesting and diverse. He would have a lot of responsibility and oversee other employees. It would be a big step up for him.

Robert arrived early for his interview, and he's been sitting in the office for ten minutes. He is filled with doubts. How many other applicants are there for the job? Does he have more experience than they do? How can he show the interviewer that he is competent and qualified? He believes he has done everything he could. He has dressed well. He has written an impressive résumé and has gotten very good letters of recommendation. He has done some research and has gotten information about National Machines so that he can ask intelligent questions. But has he done enough?

The receptionist has just announced that he may go in for his interview. As he walks into the room, he stops in surprise. His old accounting teacher, Ms. Miranda, is sitting behind the desk.

"Professor Miranda! Do you remember me?"

"Of course I do, Robert. You were one of my best students. Come in and take a seat."

1. Where is Robert?

_____

2. Why is he nervous?

_____

3. Has Robert ever had an interview before?

_____

4. What are the advantages of working for this company?

_____

5. Describe the position he's applying for.

_____

6. What is Robert worried about?

_____

7. What do you think he is wearing?

_____

8. What has he done to show the interviewer that he is qualified?

_____

9. How does Robert know the interviewer?

_____

10. Will she hire Robert?

_____

**Discussion Questions:**

1. Have you ever had a job interview?
2. How did you find out about the job?
3. What did you wear to the interview?
4. How did you feel while you were waiting for the interview?
5. What language did you speak at the interview?
6. What are some of the questions that the interviewer asked you?
7. Were you qualified for the job?
8. Did you get the job?

## Grammar Summary

The **present perfect** tells about repeated actions in the past which may be repeated in the future.

**Always** and **never** come before the main verb. **A few times, several times, from time to time,** etc., come at the end of the sentence.

| I<br>You<br>We<br>They | have | always | had | problems | with the boss. |
|---|---|---|---|---|---|
| He<br>She<br>It | has | never | | | with other workers. |

| I<br>You<br>We<br>They | have | had | problems | with the boss | a few times.<br><br>several times. |
|---|---|---|---|---|---|
| He<br>She<br>It | has | | | with other workers | from time to time. |

## Yes/No Questions:

**Has** he ever **used** a computer? Yes, he **has.**
**Have** you ever **had** a job interview? No, I **haven't.**

## UNIT 13
# VACATION PLANS

## Present Perfect with Already, Yet, and Just.

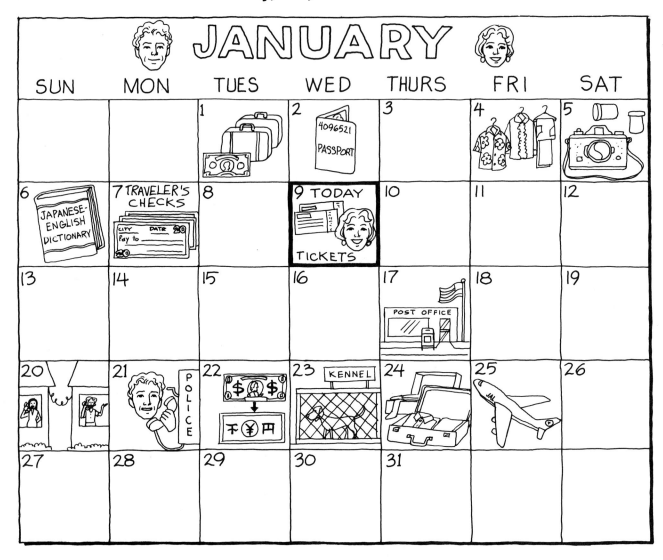

Today is January 9. On January 25, Harry and his wife, Ellen, are going to take a vacation to Japan. They've already started preparing for the trip. There are many things that they still have to do before they go.

**A.** Read each statement. Look at the calendar. Circle "T" if it is true. Circle "F" if it is false.

1. Ellen has just picked up the tickets.                    (T)      F

2. Harry and Ellen have already gone to Japan.              T        F

90

| | | |
|---|---|---|
| 3. They have already bought new luggage. | T | F |
| 4. They have already exchanged some dollars for yen. | T | F |
| 5. Harry hasn't gotten a new camera yet. | T | F |
| 6. Harry has already received his passport. | T | F |
| 7. They have already stopped the mail. | T | F |
| 8. Ellen has already taken the dog to the kennel. | T | F |
| 9. They haven't packed yet. | T | F |
| 10. They have already gotten some traveler's checks. | T | F |

**B.** Use the chart. Form sentences about the calendar.

**Example:** They haven't gone to Japan yet.

| | | | | |
|---|---|---|---|---|
| Ellen Harry | has hasn't | (already) (just) | received her passport bought new luggage stopped the mail gone to Japan packed called the police picked up the tickets gotten a new camera | (yet). |
| They | have haven't | | | |

**C.** Ask and answer questions about each picture. Use **yet.**

**Example:** Have they received their passports yet?
**Yes, they have.**

receive    go    call    pick up

take    buy    exchange    get

get    stop    pack

## WRITING

**A.** Look at the opening calendar. Complete these sentences with the correct form of the verb. Some of the sentences are negative.

| buy | get | receive |
|---|---|---|
| call | go | stop |
| exchange | pick up | take |

1. Ellen *has* already *bought* new clothes.

2. Harry _____ just _____ a Japanese-English dictionary.

3. Ellen _____ just _____ new luggage.

4. Ellen _____ already _____ her passport.

5. They _____ _____ the mail yet.

6. Harry _____ just _____ a new camera.

7. They _____ recently _____ film.

8. They _____ _____ to Japan yet.

9. They _____ _____ the dog to the kennel yet.

10. Harry _____ _____ the neighbors yet.

11. They _____ already _____ their traveler's checks.

12. They _____ _____ some dollars for yen yet.

92

**B.** It's January 17. Look at the opening calendar. Answer these questions about the calendar. Use **already**, **just**, or **yet** in your answer.

1. It's Jan. 4. Have they taken the dog to the kennel yet?

*No, they haven't taken the dog to the kennel yet.*

2. It's Jan. 2. Have they already packed?

_____

3. It's Jan. 8. Has Ellen bought new clothes yet?

_____

4. It's Jan. 20. Have they already exchanged some dollars for yen?

_____

5. It's Jan. 9. Has Ellen picked up the tickets yet?

_____

6. It's Jan. 21. Have they just gone to Japan?

_____

7. It's Jan. 3. Has Ellen already received her passport?

_____

8. It's Jan. 21. Have they called the neighbors yet?

_____

9. It's Jan. 25. Have they already packed?

_____

10. It's Jan. 26. Have they gone to Japan yet?

_____

11. It's Jan. 8. Has Harry already bought a Japanese dictionary?

_____

12. It's Jan. 18. Has Harry stopped the mail yet?

_____

**C.** It's February 1, and Harry and Ellen are in Japan. Write questions and answers about the pictures. Use **already**, **just**, and **yet**. Use the phrases in parentheses to write your questions.

| HOTEL | TOKYO TOWER | MEIJI SHRINE | SUSHI | GARDEN | GINZA SHOPPING | TODAY |
|---|---|---|---|---|---|---|
| 26 | 27 | 28 | 29 | 30 | 31 | 1 |

| 2 | 3 | 4 | 5 | 6 |
|---|---|---|---|---|
| | SHINKANSEN | HOT SPRING | KYOTO TEMPLE | DISCO |

1. (check into the hotel)

   *Have they checked into the hotel yet?* ?

   *Yes they have.* .

2. (visit Tokyo Tower)

   _____ ?

   _____ .

3. (see Meiji Shrine)

   _____ ?

   _____ .

4. (dance at a Tokyo disco)

   _____ ?

   _____ .

5. (eat sushi)

   _____ ?

   _____ .

6. (shop in the Ginza area)

_____?

_____.

7. (go to a baseball game)                                       ?

_____

_____.

8. (ride the *Shinkansen)

_____?

_____.

9. (take a bath in a hot spring)

_____?

_____.

10. (see a Japanese garden)                                      ?

_____

_____.

* an express train

**D.** Read the paragraphs. Then, answer the questions.

Harry and Ellen have been in Tokyo for five days. Today they're shopping for gifts in the Ginza shopping district. Before they left home, they exchanged $300 into yen, and they brought the rest of their money in traveler's checks. They've already spent all of their yen. Right now they're in the Mitsukoshi Department Store because Ellen wants to buy a Japanese doll for her niece.

1. Have Harry and Ellen arrived in Tokyo yet?

_____

2. How much money have they spent?

_____

3. Why have they come to Mitsukoshi Department Store?

_____

Ellen sees a beautiful doll, so she asks Harry for the traveler's checks because they're out of cash. Harry reaches into his jacket pocket to get the checks, but they're not there.

4. Has Ellen found a nice gift?

_____

5. Why did Ellen ask Harry for the traveler's checks?

_____

6. Where did Harry put the checks?

_____

When Harry sees that his checks are missing, he thinks they have just been stolen or that he has dropped them somewhere in the store. He goes to the store's "Lost and Found" office, but no one has turned them in.

7. Why hasn't Ellen bought the doll yet?

_____

8. What does Harry think has happened to the checks?

_____

Harry and Ellen go back to their hotel to see if their traveler's checks are there. When they get to the front desk, there is an envelope waiting for them. Someone has found the checks and turned them in to the manager. When Harry opens the envelope, he sees that all the checks are there.

9. Why did Harry and Ellen go back to their hotel?

_____

10. Ellen will be able to buy her niece's present today. Why is that possible?

_____

**Discussion Question:**

Have you ever had an interesting or unusual experience when you were on vacation? Tell the class about your experience.

## Grammar Summary

The present perfect tells about an action completed in the past, but the definite time is not known.

**Already** shows that an action is completed. It is used in affirmative sentences. **Already** is placed before the main verb or at the end of the sentence.

They have **already** gotten some traveler's checks.
They have gotten some traveler's checks **already**.

**Yet** shows the action has not started. It is used in negative sentences. **Yet** is placed at the end of the sentence.

Harry hasn't gotten a new camera **yet**.

**Just** shows than an action was completed a very short time ago. It is used in affirmative sentences. **Just** is placed before the main verb.

Ellen has **just** picked up the tickets.

| I<br>You<br>We<br>They | have | already | bought the tickets. |
|---|---|---|---|
| He<br>She<br>It | has | just | |

| We | haven't | bought the tickets | yet. |
|---|---|---|---|
| He | hasn't | | |

**Yes/No Questions:**

**Have** they **received** their passports yet? Yes, they **have**.
**Has** he already **bought** a Japanese dictionary? Yes, he **has**.

# UNIT 14
# AT THE DISCO

## Present Perfect Continuous

**A.** It's 11:00 at night at the Rio, a popular nightclub. Read each sentence.
Circle "T" if it is true. Circle "F" if it is false.

1. Larry has been smoking for four hours.                          T    (F)
2. Tony and Teresa have been arguing for an hour.                  T    F
3. Jeff and Karen have been eating since 9:00.                     T    F
4. Mark has been talking since 9:00.                               T    F
5. Victor has been waiting tables since 5:00.                      T    F
6. Bruce and Cheryl have been dancing for four hours.             T    F
7. Howard and Linda have been sitting at the bar since 9:00.      T    F

8. Stu has been working for six hours.       T     F

9. Loretta and Dave have been working since 10:00.       T     F

10. Kay has been working for two hours.       T     F

**B.** Circle the correct answer, **for** or **since**.

**For** tells an amount of time, e.g., the number of minutes, hours, days. **Since** tells when an action started.

| for | a half hour<br>one hour<br>three hours<br>six hours | since | 5:00<br>8:00<br>10:00<br>10:30 |
|---|---|---|---|

1. Tony has been arguing **for** / **since** 10:30.
2. Larry has been smoking **for** / **since** three hours.
3. Tom and Victor have been working **for** / **since** 5:00.
4. Kay has been working **for** / **since** 5:00.
5. Bruce and Cheryl have been dancing **for** / **since** three hours.
6. Jeff and Karen have been eating **for** / **since** three hours.
7. Stu has been making drinks **for** / **since** six hours.
8. Loretta has been singing **for** / **since** 10:30.
9. Howard and Linda have been drinking **for** / **since** one hour.
10. Anna and Mark have been talking **for** / **since** 8:00.

**C.** Use the chart. Form sentences about the disco.

**Example:** Dave and Loretta have been working for half an hour.

| Stu<br>Larry<br>Kay | has | been | working<br>smoking<br>eating<br>dancing | for | half an hour.<br>three hours.<br>six hours. |
|---|---|---|---|---|---|
| Jeff and Karen<br>Dave and Loretta<br>Cheryl and Bruce | have | | | since | 10:30.<br>8:00.<br>5:00. |

**D.** Answer these **Yes** / **No** questions about the picture.

**Example:** Has Larry been smoking for three hours?
         **Yes, he has.**

1. Has Kay been working since 5:00?
2. Has Stu been making drinks since 5:00?
3. Have Loretta and Dave been working for one hour?

4. Have Tom and Victor been working for seven hours?

5. Have Bruce and Cheryl been dancing for four hours?

6. Has Tony been arguing for two hours?

7. Has Howard been drinking since 10:00?

8. Has Karen been eating since 8:00?

9. Have Anna and Mark been talking since 8:00?

10. Have Howard and Linda been sitting at the bar for two hours?

**E.**

**Example:** How long has Dave been working as a guitar player?
**He's been working as a guitar player for eight years.**

1. How long has Stu been working as a bartender?

2. How long has Kay been working at the hatcheck?

3. How long has Loretta been working as a singer?

4. How long has Dave been working as a musician?

5. How long has Victor been working as a waiter?

6. How long has Tom been working as a waiter?

7. How long have Victor and Tom been working as waiters?

8. How long have Loretta and Dave been working as performers?

## Writing

**A.** Choose the correct verb and complete these sentences. Use **for** or **since** in each sentence.

| | | |
|---|---|---|
| argue | eat | talk |
| dance | sing | work |
| drink | smoke | |

1. Larry _has been smoking for_ three hours.

2. Tony _____ _____ _____ _____ 10:30.

3. Kay _____ _____ _____ _____ 5:00.

4. Stu _____ _____ _____ _____ six hours.

5. Loretta _____ _____ _____ _____ 10:00.

6. Tom and Victor _____ _____ _____ _____ 5:00.

7. Howard and Linda _____ _____ _____ _____ one hour.

8. Anna and Mark _____ _____ _____ _____ 8:00.

9. Jeff and Karen _____ _____ _____ _____ three hours.

10. Bruce and Cheryl _____ _____ _____ _____ three hours.

**B.** These people are working in the disco's kitchen. Write ten sentences about the picture with **for** or **since**. Decide "how long" for each activity.

1. *Ann has been chopping vegetables for an hour.*

2. _____

3. _____

4. _____

5. _____

6. _____

7. _____

8. _____

9. _____

10. _____

**C.** Complete the questions about the picture on page 98 in the present continuous or the present perfect continuous. Then, write the answers.

1. What _is_ Mark _doing_ now?

   _He's talking._ _____

   How long _has_ he _been talking_ ?

   _He's been talking since 8:00._ _____

2. What _____ Stu _____ now?

   _____

   How long _____ he _____ ?

   _____

3. What _____ Dave and Loretta _____ now?

   _____

   How long _____ they _____ ?

   _____

4. What _____ Howard and Linda _____ now?

   _____

   How long _____ they _____ ?

   _____

5. What _____ Kay _____ now?

   _____

   How long _____ she _____ ?

   _____

102

6. What _____ Larry _____ now?

_____

How long _____ he _____ ?

_____


**D.** Read this story about some of the customers at the Rio. Then, answer the questions.

My name is Stu. I'm the bartender at the Rio, a famous New York nightclub. It's Saturday night, and all of the regular customers are here. I know them all. From behind the bar I can see everything that's going on. I also know what's happening in their lives. Many of them trust me, so they come over and talk to me and tell me their problems.

For example, the man who has been standing against the pole near the bar all evening is Larry. He's been chain-smoking, one cigarette after the other, since he arrived. I think he's a little depressed tonight. He's been thinking about his girlfriend who moved to Montreal. She's been living there for three months. They write letters to each other every week, but he misses her a lot. She's supposed to come home for a visit next week. They plan to get married in several months. They've been trying to decide where they will live, here or in Montreal. Anyway, I can understand why he's sad. It's difficult to have a long-distance relationship.

Tony and Teresa met here three years ago, and they got married a year later. They are sitting at the table near the stage. That's their favorite table. They come here every Saturday night, so we reserve it for them. They sat down about an hour ago. They've been arguing ever since they came in. They argue every week when they come in, but after eating, drinking, and dancing, they go home laughing. I guess it's difficult to have a relationship when you live with someone, too.

Oh well. I love my work. I've been working here for twelve years. I've met many interesting people, and some have become my good friends. We are like a big, happy family.

1. Has Stu been working at the Rio for a long time?

_____

2. Where is he standing now?

_____

3. How does he know about the customers' lives?

_____

4. Who is the man standing against the pole?

_____

5. What has Larry been doing all night?

_____

6. Where does his girlfriend live?

_____

7. When did she move there?

_____

8. How does he feel about her?

_____

9. What is she going to do soon?

_____

10. How long have Tony and Teresa been married?

_____

11. How often do they come to the Rio?

_____

12. Where is their table?

_____

13. What happens every Saturday night?

_____

14. According to Stu, is it easy to have a relationship?

_____

15. Why does Stu love his work?

_____

**Discussion Questions:**

1. Have you ever been to a disco?
2. Do you like to dance?
3. Have you ever met anyone at a disco?
4. What's a good place to meet people?
5. Have you ever had a long-distance relationship?
6. Are you still involved in this relationship?
7. If not, how long did it last?
8. How do you relax on the weekends?

# Grammar Summary

The **present perfect continuous** talks about an action that started in the past and continues into the present. The action is not complete.

**Statements:**

| I You We They | have haven't | | talking dancing | for | one hour. three hours. six hours. |
|---|---|---|---|---|---|
| | | been | | | |
| He She It | has hasn't | | eating | since | 5:00. 8:00. 10:00. |

**Questions:**

| Have | I you we they | | talking dancing | for | one hour? three hours? six hours? |
|---|---|---|---|---|---|
| | | been | | | |
| Has | he she it | | eating | since | 5:00? 8:00? 10:00? |

**How long Questions:**

How long **have** they **been dancing**?
How long **has** he **been working** there?

# THE NEW PARENTS

## Future Time Clauses

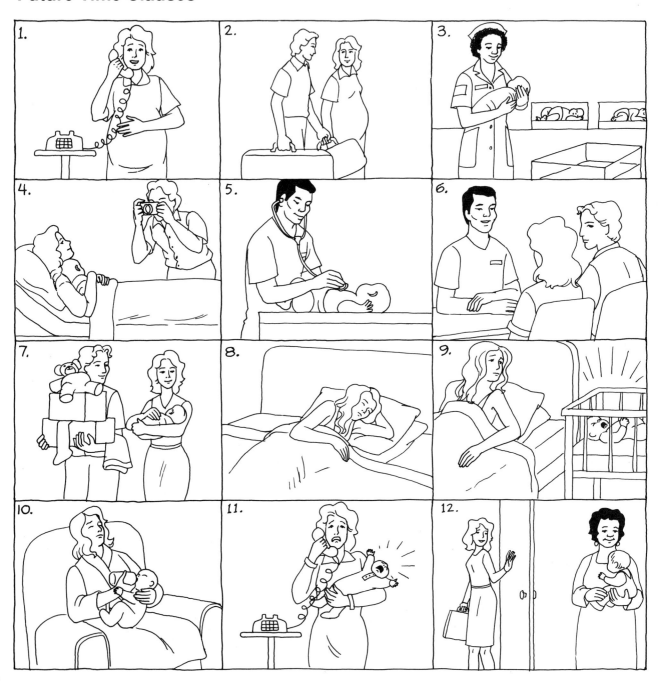

**A.** Susan and Paul are expecting their first baby. Look at the pictures and listen to your teacher talk about their plans. After you listen two or three times, retell the story.

**B.** Read each sentence.  Then, write the number of the matching picture on the line.

_____ a. Before they leave the hospital, Paul will take a lot of photographs.

_____ b. When they go to the hospital, Paul will carry Susan's suitcase.

_____ c. After they get home, Susan will take a long nap.

_____ d. As soon as Susan's labor pains start, she will call the doctor.

_____ e. While they are in the hospital, the doctor will check the baby.

_____ f. Susan will sleep until the baby cries.

_____ g. Susan will feed the baby when he* cries.

_____ h. After the baby is born, the nurse will put him* in the nursery.

_____ i. Susan will call her mother if she needs help.

_____ j. When they leave the hospital, they will take their presents home.

_____ k. If the baby has a problem, the doctor will talk to Paul and Susan.

_____ l. Susan will stay home from work until the baby is one year old.

*People may talk about an unborn baby as male or female. Some people use **it**.

**C.** Circle the correct word.

1. Susan will stay home from work (**until**)/ **before**  the baby is one year old.
2. She'll call her mother **before** / **if**  she needs help.
3. Susan will feed the baby **when** / **before**  he cries.
4. She will sleep **until** / **if**  the baby cries.
5. Susan will take a rest **after** / **if**  they get home.
6. **When** / **After**  they leave the hospital, they will take their presents home.
7. **If** / **After**  the baby has a problem, the doctor will talk to them.
8. **While** / **After**  they are in the hospital, the doctor will check the baby.
9. **Before** / **If**  they leave the hospital, Paul will take many photographs.
10. **After** / **Before**  the baby is born, the nurse will put him in the nursery.

**D.** Answer these questions about Susan and Paul's plans.

1. Whom will Susan call as soon as her labor pains start?
2. Where will the nurse put the baby after he's born?
3. When will Paul take photographs?
4. What will the doctor do while they are in the hospital?
5. How long will Susan stay home?
6. When will Susan take a nap?
7. How long will Susan sleep?
8. When will Susan feed the baby?
9. What will the doctor do if the baby has a problem?
10. What will Susan do if she needs help?

## Writing

**A.** Complete the sentences with the correct form of the verb.

| | | | |
|---|---|---|---|
| be | feed | leave | start |
| call | get | need | stay |
| carry | go | put | take |
| cry | have | sleep | talk |

1. Susan _will stay_ home from work until the baby ___is___ one year old.

2. Susan _____ until the baby _____ .

3. The doctor _____ to Paul and Susan if the baby _____ a problem.

4. Susan _____ a long rest after she _____ home.

5. Paul _____ the suitcase when they _____ to the hospital.

6. If Susan _____ help with the baby, she _____ her mother.

7. When the baby _____ , Paul _____ the bottle and Susan _____ the baby.

8. Before they _____ the hospital, Paul _____ many photographs.

9. As soon as Susan's labor pains _____ , she _____ the doctor.

10. After the baby _____ born, the nurse _____ him in the nursery.

**B.** Combine these sentences with the words in parentheses.

1. The baby is born.
   Paul will call their parents. (as soon as)

   *Paul will call their parents as soon as the baby is born.*

2. Paul will give cigars to all his friends.
   He goes back to work. (when)

3. Susan and Paul will receive cards and presents.
   Susan is in the hospital. (while)

4. Susan will write thank-you notes.
   She's not too tired. (if)

5. The nurse will show Susan and Paul how to change the baby.
   They leave the hospital. (before)

6. Susan is in the hospital.
   She will take a "baby bath" class. (while)

7. Susan is in the hospital.
   Paul will bring her flowers. (while)

8. They drive home.
They will put the baby in a car seat. (before)

_____

_____

9. They get home.
Friends and relatives will visit them. (after)

_____

_____

10. They won't get any rest.
They turn off the telephone. (until)

_____

_____

**C.** Complete these sentences about Susan and Paul and the baby. The baby is now one year old.

1. Susan and Paul will get a baby-sitter when *they go to a movie.*

_____

2. They'll take the baby to the doctor when _____

_____

3. Susan will buy shoes for the baby after _____

_____

4. Paul will change the baby's diaper as soon as _____

_____

5. The baby will wear diapers until _____

_____

6. The baby won't sleep through the night until _____

_____

7. The baby will stay with his grandmother when _____

_____

8. They will have another baby after _____

_____

9. Paul will take many pictures of the baby when _____

_____

10. Susan will return to work when _____

_____

**D.** Complete these sentences with **so. . .that**. Choose an adjective from the box below.

| | | | |
|---|---|---|---|
| cold | exhausted | hungry | tired |
| cute | expensive | proud | |
| excited | happy | small | |

1. The baby is *so hungry that* he can't go to sleep.

2. Susan is _____ _____ _____ she's going to fall asleep right now.

3. Paul is _____ _____ _____ he's going to call everyone he knows.

4. Paul is _____ _____ _____ he's going to take photographs of the baby to work.

5. The baby is _____ _____ _____ people will stop and say "What a beautiful baby!"

6. The new parents are _____ _____ _____ they'll have a party to celebrate.

7. Susan is _____ _____ _____ she's going to call her mother to help her take care of the baby.

8. The apartment is _____ _____ _____ they will have to move in a couple of years.

9. It is _____ _____ _____ they will have to dress the baby in warm clothes when they take him for a walk.

10. Baby food is _____ _____ _____ Susan will prepare her own baby food.

**E.** Read this story about Susan and Paul. Then, answer the questions.

Susan and Paul are in the hospital now. They are in the labor room. Susan has been in labor for sixteen hours, but the baby has not moved down. The doctor says that she will have to have a Cesarean operation. Susan is relieved because she has been in a lot of pain, but Paul is nervous. While the nurses move Susan to the delivery room and prepare her for the operation, Paul will take a short break. When he leaves the labor room, he will go downstairs to the cafeteria to get a quick cup of coffee. He won't be able to relax until the baby arrives. Before he goes upstairs to the waiting room, he is going to smoke a cigarette. He quit smoking two years ago, but he is so nervous that smoking is the only thing that can calm him down. As soon as he finishes his cigarette, he's going to run up to the waiting room. He wants to be there when the baby is born.

1. When did Susan's labor begin?

   _____.

2. What's the problem?

   _____.

3. What will the doctor do?

   _____.

4. How do Susan and Paul feel?

   _____.

5. Where is Paul going to get a cup of coffee?

   _____.

6. Where is the doctor going to perform the Cesarean?

   _____.

7. When will Paul relax?

   _____.

8. When will he smoke a cigarette?

   _____.

9. Why does he need a cigarette?

   _____.

10. When is Paul going to return to the waiting room?

   _____.

# Grammar Summary

Time clauses begin with words such as **when**, **if**, **before**, **after**, and **as soon as**. A clause has a subject and a verb.

In a future time clause, the verb in the main clause is in the future tense. The verb in the time clause is in the present tense.

| Main Clause | Time Clause |
|---|---|
| Paul **will take** many pictures<br>Susan **will call** her mother | before they **leave** the hospital.<br>if she **needs** help. |

| Time Clause | Main Clause |
|---|---|
| Before they **leave** the hospital,*<br>If Susan **needs** help, | Paul **will take** many pictures.<br>she **will call** her mother. |

*Note: When the time clause is first, use a comma to separate it from the main clause.

**Should**

HELEN            CAROL

| | |
|---|---|
| 1. STEVEN | 2. PAUL |
| 3. 3 months | 4. 1 year |
| 5. | 6. |
| 7. | 8. |
| 9. DISPOSABLE DIAPERS | 10. |
| 11. | 12. |
| 13. | 14. |
| 15. | 16. |
| 17. | 18. |

**A.** Susan and Paul just had a baby boy. Their mothers are thrilled with their new grandson. They are giving Susan and Paul a lot of advice, but they have different opinions about everything. Look at the pictures and listen to your teacher talk about the pictures. After you listen two or three times, retell the story.

**B.** Read each sentence. Whose opinion is it? Write **Helen** or **Carol** on the line after each statement.

1. Susan should go back to work in three months. _____

2. Susan and Paul should feed the baby every four hours. _____

3. They should use disposable diapers. _____

4. Susan should nurse the baby. _____

5. They should pick up the baby every time he cries. _____

6. They should give the baby a pacifier. _____

7. They should bottle-feed the baby. _____

8. The baby should wear shoes. _____

9. They should name the baby Paul. _____

10. The baby should sleep in his own bedroom. _____

**C.** Use the chart. Form sentences about Helen's and Carol's opinions.

**Example:** Carol thinks they shouldn't give the baby a pacifier.

| | | | nurse | the baby. |
|---|---|---|---|---|
| Helen thinks | Susan | should | use | disposable diapers. |
| | | | give | the baby a pacifier. |
| Carol thinks | they | shouldn't | feed | the baby every four hours. |
| | | | pick up | the baby when he cries. |

**D.** Answer these questions about the grandmothers' opinions.

**Example:** According to Helen, should Susan nurse the baby?
**No, she shouldn't. She should bottle-feed him.**

According to Helen,

1. When should Susan feed the baby?
2. What kind of diapers should they use?
3. Should they give the baby a pacifier?
4. What should they name the baby?
5. Should they pick him up every time he cries?

According to Carol,

6. What should they name the baby?
7. Where should the baby sleep?
8. Should the baby wear shoes?
9. When should Susan go back to work?
10. Should they give the baby a pacifier?


## Writing

**A.** Give **your** opinion in each sentence below. Use **should** or **shouldn't**.

1. Parents _____ name their child after themselves.

2. A new mother _____ stay home from work for_____.

3. Mothers _____ nurse their babies.

4. A parent _____ pick up the baby every time it cries.

5. Parents _____ use disposable diapers.

6. The new baby _____ sleep in its parents' bedroom.

7. A parent _____ feed the baby when it cries.

8. A baby _____ wear shoes.

9. A parent _____ give the baby a pacifier.

10. A father _____ change the baby's diapers.

**B.** Use the chart. Ask and answer ten questions about the new baby.

| Should | Susan<br><br>Paul<br><br>they | stay<br>feed<br>pick up<br>change<br>bottle-feed<br>use | home with the baby?<br>the baby every four hours?<br>the baby when he cries?<br>the baby's diapers?<br>the baby?<br>a car seat?<br>a playpen? |
|---|---|---|---|

1. *Should Susan use a car seat?* _____ *Yes, she should.*

2. _____ _____

3. _____ _____

4. _____ _____

5. _____ _____

6. _____ _____

7. _____ _____

8. _____ _____

9. _____ _____

10. _____ _____

**C.** Complete these sentences with **should** for advice or opinion, or with **have to** / **has to** for obligation.

1. A parent *has to* get immunizations for a baby.

2. A parent _____ take a baby for walks.

3. New parents _____ give their child a name.

4. Parents _____ buy toys for their baby.

5. New parents _____ fill out an application for a birth certificate.

6. Parents _____ share the responsibility for taking care of their children.

7. In most states, parents _____ put a child in a car seat.

8. A doctor _____ examine the new baby in the hospital.

9. Parents _____ enjoy their children.

10. If possible, grandparents _____ help with the new baby.

117

**D.** Steven is now eight months old. Read each situation, and then give Susan and Paul some advice about their problems.

Steven is crawling, and Susan has to watch him every minute. It's difficult to do anything around the house. Simple things, like making dinner or taking a shower, are becoming major problems. Last week Susan bought a playpen for Steven, but he doesn't want to spend any time in it. When Susan puts him in the playpen, he cries. Susan needs time to do housework and to make dinner, and she wants Steven to stay in his playpen.

1. Why does Susan have to watch Steven every minute?

   _____

2. Does Steven like his playpen?

   _____

3. Should Susan make Steven use the playpen?

   _____

4. Give Susan two suggestions about the playpen.

   _____

   _____

Paul's parents came for dinner last Saturday. Steven ate dinner with them. Paul put various soft foods on the tray of the baby's high chair—peas, slices of banana, and pieces of cheese—and Steven fed himself. The result, of course, was a terrible mess, with food on Steven's face and hair and on the floor. Paul's mother wiped Steven's face every minute, and his father picked up every piece of food from the floor as soon as Steven dropped it. Paul's parents didn't enjoy their meal. Paul explained that they believe in self-feeding, but his parents don't agree.

1. Did Paul feed the baby with a spoon?

   _____

2. How did Paul's parents feel during the dinner?

   _____

3. What should Paul do the next time his parents come for dinner?

   _____

4. Give Paul two suggestions about dinnertime and his parents.

   _____

   _____

**Discussion Questions:**

1. Should a new mother bottle-feed her baby?
2. What kind of diapers should parents use?
3. Should a baby wear shoes?
4. Should parents pick up a new baby every time it cries?
5. Where should a new baby sleep, in the parents' room or in a separate room?
6. How often should parents feed a new baby?
7. Should parents give their baby a pacifier?
8. When should a baby start solid food?
9. When should the new mother go back to work?
10. Should parents name their children after themselves?

# Grammar Summary

**Should** expresses opinion or advice.

### Statements:

| Susan They | should shouldn't | use disposable diapers. feed the baby every four hours. |
|---|---|---|

### Yes/No Questions:

| Should | Susan they | use disposable diapers? feed the baby every four hours? |
|---|---|---|

# HAPPY BIRTHDAY

**Could**

**A.** Olga is trying to decide what to get her mother for her 50th birthday. David and the children are giving suggestions. Read each sentence. Then, write the number of the matching picture on the line.

_____ a. You could take her out to dinner.

_____ b. You could give her a vacation to Hawaii.

_____ c. You could get her tickets to a show.

_____ d. You could paint her kitchen.

_____ e. You could buy her a camera.

_____ f. You could take her to the city for the day.

_____ g. You could give her a year's membership to a fitness club.

_____ h. You could give her a gift certificate to her favorite beauty salon.

_____ i. You could throw her a surprise party.

_____ j. You could make her a dress.

**B.** Give each person two or three gift suggestions.

**Example:**
My son's birthday is next week. He's going to be 15.
You could get him tickets to a baseball game.

1.
Next week is my wife's birthday.

2.
Next month is my Mom and Dad's 25th wedding anniversary.

3.
My brother is going to be 23 on Friday.

4.
My sister is graduating from high school next month.

5.
My roommate's birthday is in two weeks.

**C.** Read the suggestions in Exercise A. Change the suggestion; begin with **Why don't you.** Then, give a response from the charts below.

| | |
|---|---|
| Yes, I could.<br>That's a great idea.<br>I like that. | She already has _____ .<br>She hates _____ .<br>No, I don't think so. |

**Example:** Why don't you buy her a camera?
        That's a great idea!
          or
    She already has one.

**D.** Complete these sentences with a birthday gift suggestion for each person.

    **Example:** She plays tennis a lot, so…
        She plays tennis a lot, so you could give her a can of tennis balls.
        She plays tennis a lot, so why don't you give her a can of tennis balls?

1. He just bought a new VCR, so…
2. She reads all the time, so…
3. He likes to take pictures of his family, so…
4. He's a real baseball fan, so…
5. It's hard for them to go out because the baby is so little, so…
6. They love Italian food, so…
7. She loves your homemade bread, so…
8. She enjoys cooking, so…
9. They're going on a trip, so…
10. He loves to do things around the house, so…

## Writing

**A.** Give each person a gift suggestion. Use an expression from the first box and a verb from the second box.

| | | | | |
|---|---|---|---|---|
| You could<br>Why don't you…? | baby-sit<br>buy | get<br>give | make<br>send | take<br>throw |

1. Why don't you _____get_____ him a ring.
2. _____ _____ her flowers.
3. _____ _____ them out to the new French restaurant in town.
4. _____ _____ her a surprise party.
5. _____ _____ them a vacation in Bermuda.
6. _____ _____ for their children while they go away for the weekend.

7. _____ _____ her a card.

8. _____ _____ him to a concert.

9. _____ _____ her a birthday cake.

10. _____ _____ her a subscription to a magazine.

**B.** Give two suggestions to each person.

1. Next week is my sister's birthday. She's going to be twelve. I have five dollars to buy her something.

   *You could buy her a book.*

   *Why don't you take her to the movies?*

2. Next month is my Dad's birthday. He lives overseas. The postage is expensive, so I want to send him something small and light.

   _____

   _____

3. This summer is my parents' 40th wedding anniversary. My brother and I want to do something very special.

   _____

   _____

4. My father is getting old. It's his birthday soon. I'd like to do something special in his house, something he can't do himself.

   _____

   _____

5. Next week is my boss's birthday. I'm not going to buy him a present, but I'd like to say "Happy Birthday" in a small way.

   _____

   _____

**C.** Read each situation. Then, answer the questions.

1. Mrs. Lyle is 84 years old and lives alone in a small house next to David and Olga. She has no children. David and Olga talk to her and occasionally invite her to a barbecue or dinner at their house. Her 85th birthday is next month.

   a. Is Mrs. Lyle married?

   _____

   b. Should David and Olga throw her a surprise birthday party? Why or why not?

   _____

   c. What could they give her as a present?

   _____

2. Kathy is going to be twelve next week. She wants a computer, but her parents don't have enough money to buy her one this year.

   a. What should her parents do?

   _____

   b. What could they give Kathy instead?

   _____

3. Michael and Patty live in California. They're celebrating their first wedding anniversary in June. Michael wants to fly to Hawaii. Kathy thinks they should save that money for a new car.

   a. What does Michael think they should do?

   _____

   b. Who is more practical?

   _____

   c. How else could they celebrate their anniversary?

   _____

   d. What do you think they should do?

   _____

# Grammar Summary

**Could** and **Why don't you** express a suggestion.

| You | could | buy | her<br>him<br>them | a camera. |
|-----|-------|-----|--------------------|-----------|

| Why don't you | buy | her<br>him<br>them | a camera? |
|---------------|-----|--------------------|-----------|

# ■ UNIT 18 ■
# COLLEGE

## Infinitives

**A.** Teresa wants to go to college, but she doesn't have enough money. Listen to your teacher read these sentences about her plans. Each sentence has a verb that is followed by an infinitive. Fill in the infinitive form. Then, draw a box around the first verb.

**Example:** Teresa can't afford   *to go*   to college.

1. Her parents can't afford _____ her enough money.

2. Teresa managed _____ some money.

3. She still needed _____ some more.

4. She decided _____ a loan from a bank.

5. She didn't expect _____ the loan.

126

6. She waited _____ from the bank.

7. The bank agreed _____ her a student loan.

8. She decided _____ the loan.

9. She promised _____ back the loan within ten years.

10. Her grandmother offered _____ her books.

**B.** Circle the correct form of the verb.

1. Teresa wants **to go / going** to college.

2. She plans **attends / to attend** school in September.

3. She decided **went / to go** to the community college.

4. She intends transfer / to transfer to the state university after two years.

5. She'll try **to get / get** a part-time job at school.

6. Teresa likes **to study / studied.**

7. She plans **studies / to study** art.

8. She expects **to do / doing** well in school.

9. She would like **be / to be** an art therapist.

10. She volunteered **worked / to work** as an assistant to the art therapist at the hospital.

**C.** Use the chart to form sentences about Teresa and her college plans.

**Example:** Teresa would like to study art.

| | decided<br>wants<br>hopes<br>would like<br>can't afford<br>arranged<br>agreed | | go<br>study<br>send<br>give<br>get<br>borrow<br>take<br>pay back | | to college.<br>art.<br>money.<br>a loan.<br>the loan. |
|---|---|---|---|---|---|
| Teresa<br><br>Her parents<br><br>The bank | | to | | (her) | |

**D.** Answer these questions about Teresa's college plans.

1. What can't Teresa afford to do?

2. What did she decide to apply for?

3. What did the bank agree to do?

4. What did she promise to do within ten years?

5. What does she plan to do in September?

6. What did her grandmother offer to buy?

7. What does she plan to study?

8. What would Teresa like to be?

9. When does she plan to start school?

10. Where did she volunteer to work?

**E.** These verbs are followed by **an object + an infinitive.**

| | | |
|---|---|---|
| advise | encourage | remind tell |
| ask | expect | require |

Read each sentence, then say it again using the verb in parentheses. Use a **verb + object + infinitive.**

**Examples:**

Teresa's counselor said, "Go to college." (encourage)
He <u>encouraged her to go</u> to college.
Teresa said to her counselor, "Please help me with the application form."
She <u>asked him to help</u> her with the application form.

1. Teresa's art teacher said, "You should be an art therapist." (encourage)
2. Her parents said, "Go to the state university." (advise)
3. The counselor said, "Take your SATs." (remind)
4. He said, "Apply early." (tell)
5. The college said, "Pay a $25 application fee." (require)
6. Teresa said to her counselor, "Please check my application." (ask)
7. Her parents said, "Apply for financial aid." (advise)
8. The college said, "Send your high school transcript." (require)
9. The counselor said, "You will do well in college." (expect)
10. He said, "Study hard." (advise)

## Writing

**A.** Complete these sentences with the infinitive.

| | | | | |
|---|---|---|---|---|
| attend | begin | buy | give | study |
| be | borrow | get | go | work |

1. Teresa wants ___*to go*___ to college.

2. Her parents can't afford _____ her much money.

3. Teresa needed _____ some money.

4. Teresa arranged _____ a loan from a bank.

5. Teresa intends _____ part-time at college.

6. Her grandmother offered _____ her books.

7. Teresa plans _____ an art therapist.

8. She decided _____ a community college for two years.

9. She expects _____ school in the fall.

10. She hopes _____ art.

**B.** Read each situation. Write a sentence about it, using the verb in parentheses.

1. Teresa doesn't have enough money to go to college.   (can't afford)

   *Teresa can't afford to go to college.*

2. Teresa will work part time when she attends college.   (decide)

   _____

3. Her parents said she should go to college.   (encourage)

   _____

4. She has some money in the bank.   (manage)

   _____

5. She's going to work in a hospital one day a week.   (volunteer)

   _____

6. Her grandmother said, "I will give you money for books."   (offer)

   _____

7. Her counselor told her she should get a loan from a bank.   (advise)

   _____

8. She will start school in September.   (plan)

   _____

9. Teresa thinks she can finish school in five years.   (intend)

   _____

10. The school told her that she had to take a placement test.   (require)

    _____

**C.** Complete these sentences about yourself.

1. I want _____ .

2. I like _____ .

3. I decided _____ .

4. I expect _____ .

5. I tried _____ .

6. I plan _____ .

7. I hope _____ .

8. I can't afford _____ .

9. I would like _____ .

10. I need _____ .

**D.** Read the story, and then answer the questions.

Teresa is looking around the large, spacious art room at the Cliffside Mental Health Center. The room is airy and colorful; brightly colored art projects decorate the walls. Classical music is playing on the stereo. The room is busy. Several patients are sitting around the room, getting ready to work on art projects. They are participating in an art therapy workshop. Emily, the art therapist, has asked the patients to arrange several small pieces of paper into the shape of a house. The patients are learning to express themselves by working on various art projects. After they work on this creative art task, they will discuss their feelings about what they have created.

Some of the patients hesitate to draw. They are afraid to draw something that is not perfect. Others refuse to draw, but Emily encourages them to do the best they can and not to worry. Emily observes and analyzes the patients' behavior and art projects. She also listens to how the patients communicate. Then she writes treatment plans as part of a total therapy program.

Teresa is going to work as Emily's assistant every Friday morning while she's in college. Teresa will help set up the art supplies before the patients come in. When the patients come in for their art therapy groups, Teresa is expected to help them. She'll encourage the patients with their projects, get supplies, display art work, and help clean up. This could be a very exciting and rewarding job. Teresa is looking forward to working here.

1. What does Teresa see and hear in the art room?

_____

2. What do the patients plan to work on?

_____

3. Who is Emily?

_____

4. What does she want the patients to do?

_____

5. Do all of the patients like to draw?

_____

6. What will the patients do when they finish working on their projects?

_____

7. What is the purpose of an art therapy workshop?

_____

8. What has Teresa decided to do on Fridays?

_____

9. What is Teresa going to do before the class begins?

_____

10. What is Teresa expected to do while the patients are working on their projects?

_____

## Grammar Summary

An infinitive = **to** + the simple form of the verb. A list of verbs that take the infinitive is in the appendix.

| Laura | wants<br>decided<br>would like | to study | art. |
|-------|-------------------------------|----------|------|

# A CHANGED MAN

## Gerunds

**A.** Listen to your teacher read these sentences about Spike. He robbed a jewelry store and is now in jail. Each sentence has a verb that is followed by a gerund. Fill in the gerund form. Then, draw a circle around the first verb.

1. Spike (can't stand) *being* _____ behind bars.

2. He misses _____ with his friends.

3. He keeps _____ to get early parole.

4. He hates _____ prison food.

5. He appreciates _____ mail.

6. Spike avoids _____ into trouble.

7. He anticipates _____ out soon.

8. Spike admitted _____ into the jewelry store.

9. He regrets _____ to his friends.

10. He is considering _____ up his life of crime.

**B.** Circle the correct verb.

1. I'm tired of **be** / **(being)** behind bars.
2. I'm considering **giving up** / **give up** my life of crime.
3. I started **read** / **reading** law books in prison.
4. I quit **smoked** / **smoking.**
5. I spend my day **work** / **working** in the prison library.
6. I have finished **studying** / **to study** for my high school diploma.
7. They are teaching me computer skills, so I practice **typing** / **to type** everyday.
8. I recommend not **lead** / **leading** a life of crime.
9. I can't help **worries** / **worrying** about the future.
10. I enjoy **have** / **having** visitors.

**C.** Answer these questions, using the words in parentheses.

**Example:** What does Spike appreciate receiving? (cookies)
       **He appreciates receiving cookies.**

| | |
|---|---|
| 1. What else does Spike appreciate receiving? | (telephone calls) |
| 2. What can't he stand? | (live in a small cell) |
| 3. What does he admit? | (steal the jewelry) |
| 4. What does he miss? | (see his family) |
| 5. What does he practice everyday? | (use the computer) |
| 6. What does he avoid doing? | (talk to other inmates) |
| 7. What does he regret? | (break into the store) |
| 8. What is he considering? | (go straight) |
| 9. What is he tired of? | (not go outside) |
| 10. What does he enjoy? | (read his books) |

**D.** Use the chart to form sentences about Spike.

**Example:** He appreciates receiving homemade food.

| He | is tired of<br>can't stand<br>misses<br>appreciates<br>anticipates<br>avoids | being<br>eating<br>speaking to<br>getting<br>receiving | in jail.<br>prison food.<br>his friends.<br>homemade food.<br>mail.<br>out soon.<br>early parole.<br>the other inmates.<br>into trouble. |
|---|---|---|---|

## Writing

**A.** Choose the correct verb. Write it in the gerund form.

| | | | | |
|---|---|---|---|---|
| eat | lead | rob | smoke | type |
| get | read | see | talk | worry |

1. He quit *smoking*.

2. He misses _____ his family.

3. He admits _____ the jewelry store.

4. He avoids _____ into trouble in prison.

5. He started _____ law books in the prison library.

6. He regrets _____ a life of crime.

7. He can't help _____ about the future.

8. He enjoys _____ to visitors.

9. He practices_____ for his computer course.

10. He can't stand _____ prison food.

**B.** Complete these sentences about Spike and about yourself.

1. Spike can't stand *being in jail* _____.

2. I can't stand _____.

3. Spike can't help _____.

4. I can't help _____.

5. Spike appreciates _____.

6. I appreciate _____.

7. Spike spends his time _____.

8. I spend my time _____.

9. Spike is considering _____.

10. I am considering _____.

11. Spike regrets _____.

12. I regret _____.

**C.** Write these sentences again, using the verb in parentheses **and a gerund.**

1. He completed his studies for his high school diploma.   (finish)

   *He finished studying for his high school diploma.*

2. He thinks he is going to give up his life of crime.   (consider)

   _____

3. He doesn't drink anymore.   (quit)

   _____

4. He doesn't like to eat the prison food.   (can't stand)

   _____

5. He began to read books in the prison library.   (start)

   _____

6. He said he stole the jewelry.   (admit)

   _____

7. He is sorry he listened to his friends.   (regret)

   _____

8. He doesn't like working in the prison library anymore.   (be tired of)

   _____

**D.** Read this story about Tina. After reading the story, circle all the **verb +
gerund** forms. Then, answer the questions.

Spike tried to rob a jewelry store while his girlfriend, Tina, waited for
him in the car. But they weren't lucky. After the police caught Spike and
Tina, they were found guilty and the judge sentenced Spike to go to jail for
two years. However, the judge had a different idea for Tina. Since this was
Tina's first arrest and she denied knowing anything about Spike's plans to
rob the store, the judge gave her a choice. Either she could go to jail for a
year, or the court could place her under house arrest for two years. The
judge advised going under house arrest. Tina listened to his advice and
decided not to go to jail.

Now she is "serving time" in her house. There are many restrictions.
She must stay home all the time except when she has to go to work. The
judge gave her a job working with teenagers in a drug clinic. She is "paying"
for her crime by giving service to the community. She doesn't mind working
there. She feels that she is doing something useful. She is also grateful that
she was able to avoid going to jail, even though she doesn't enjoy staying
home all the time.

Sometimes she feels like going to the movies, but she would risk going
to jail. The parole officers check up on her frequently. They come to the
door and phone her several times a day. She can't help thinking about
leaving her house, but she doesn't dare to go. If she isn't home when they
check, she has to go to jail. So she spends her day cleaning, cooking,
reading, writing, and knitting. The weeks go by quickly, but the weekends
seem like they will never end.

1. Who's Spike?

   _____

2. How long is Spike going to be in jail?

   _____

3. Has Tina ever been arrested before?

   _____

4. Why did the judge give Tina a choice?

   _____

5. Did she admit knowing anything about the crime?

   _____

6. What is "house arrest"?

   _____

7. When can she leave her house?

   _____

8. Where did she start working?

_____

9. How does she feel about working?

_____

10. How does she feel about staying home all the time?

_____

11. What does she miss?

_____

12. What is she tired of?

_____

## Grammar Summary

A gerund = the simple form of the verb + **ing.** A list of verbs that take the gerund is in the appendix.

| | | | |
|---|---|---|---|
| He | appreciates | getting | visitors. |
| | enjoys | | mail. |

# A PRODUCT MAP

## Present Passive

**A.** Look at this map of the western part of the United States and answer these questions.

1. Find California. Which state is located north of California?
2. Find Kansas. Which state is located west of Kansas?
3. Find South Dakota. Which state is located north of South Dakota?
4. Find Arizona. Which state is located east of Arizona?
5. Find Montana. Which state is located south of Montana?
6. Find Minnesota. Which state is located south of Minnesota?
7. Find New Mexico. Which state is located north of New Mexico?
8. Find Arkansas. Which state is located west of Arkansas?
9. Find Utah. Which state is located south of Utah?
10. Find Nebraska. Which state is located east of Nebraska?

**B.** Look at the product map. Circle "T" if the sentence is **true**. Circle "F" if it is **false**.

1. Grapes are grown in California.                          Ⓣ      F
2. Silver is mined in Kansas.                               T      F
3. Potatoes are grown in New Mexico.                        T      F
4. Farm equipment is manufactured in South Dakota.         T      F
5. Turkeys are raised in Utah.                              T      F
6. Shrimp in caught in Texas.                               T      F
7. Aerospace equipment is manufactured in Texas.           T      F
8. Copper is mined in Utah.                                 T      F
9. Rubber tires are manufactured in Oklahoma.              T      F
10. Hogs are raised in Missouri.                            T      F

**C.** Use the chart to form sentences about the product map.

**Example:** Silver isn't mined in Iowa.

| Corn Cotton Tuna Shrimp Silver Farm equipment Natural gas | is  isn't | caught  grown  manufactured | in | Montana. New Mexico. Iowa. Washington. Texas. |
|---|---|---|---|---|
| Grapes Apples Chickens Glass products Sheep | are  aren't | mined  raised | | Arkansas. California. Nevada. South Dakota. |

**D.** Circle the correct form of the verb.

1. Farmers (grow)/ **are grown** corn in Texas.
2. Gold **mines / is mined** in South Dakota.
3. Rubber tires **manufacture / are manufactured** in Oklahoma.
4. Workers **mine / are mined** uranium in Nebraska.
5. Turkeys **raise / are raised** in Minnesota.
6. Farmers **grow / are grown** lettuce in Arizona.
7. Iron ore **mines / is mined** in Wyoming.
8. Workers **manufacture / are manufactured** computers in Minnesota.
9. Fishermen **catch / is caught** salmon in Oregon.
10. Rice **is grown / are grown** in Louisiana.

## Writing

**A.** Complete these sentences with the correct form of the verb.

| | |
|---|---|
| catch | mine |
| grow | raise |
| manufacture | |

1. Copper _is mined_ in Utah.

2. Corn _____ in Iowa.

3. Chemical products _____ in Louisiana.

4. Chickens _____ in Arkansas.

5. Grapes _____ in California.

6. Shrimp _____ in Texas.

7. Farm equipment _____ in South Dakota.

8. Turkeys _____ in Minnesota.

9. Iron ore _____ in Wyoming.

10. Rice _____ in Louisiana.

**B.** Write the question for each answer.

1. _Where are apples grown_ ? In Washington.

2. _____ ? In Missouri.

3. _____ ? Computers are.

4. _____ ? Cattle are.

5. _____? In Wyoming.

6. _____? Barley is.

7. _____? In Kansas.

8. _____? Silver is.

9. _____? Rubber tires are.

10. _____? In Arizona.

**C.** What is each product made from? Where is the original product from? Write two or more sentences about each product.

1. *Wine is made from grapes. Grapes are grown in California.*

2. *Jewelry is made from gold. Gold is mined in South Dakota.*

3. _____

4. _____

5. _____

6. _____

7. _____

8. _____

9. _____

10. _____

141

**D.** Read this story about wine. Then, answer the questions.

Wine is a light alcoholic beverage made from grapes. In many countries, it is served with the evening meal or it is used in the cooking process. It is also used to celebrate special occasions, such as weddings and holidays.

Grapes are grown on vines. As the grapes ripen, they are carefully checked to determine the right time for picking, usually in the late summer or early fall. Wines are labeled by the year in which they are picked. Some years are considered superior because of the excellent growing conditions, warm days, and average rainfall.

After they are picked, the grapes are crushed mechanically. Some home wine makers still crush grapes the old-fashioned way, by foot. The natural wine yeast on the grape skin ferments the wine, changing the grape sugar into alcohol and carbon dioxide. The juice from the grapes is then pumped into tanks, where the fermentation process continues. White wine is fermented without the skins; red wine is fermented with the skins.

After fermentation, the wine is aged. It is poured into storage containers. Fine wine is usually aged in small oak barrels for up to nine months. Table wine is usually aged in large steel tanks for a much shorter time, often just a few weeks. From time to time, the wine is pumped from one tank to another to remove the small particles that have settled in the bottom of the tank. Finally, the wine is poured into bottles and stored in a cool, dark place.

The two most popular wines for mealtime are red and white. Red wine has a stronger flavor. It is served with heavier foods, such as beef or spaghetti, or with spicy food. Red wine is served at room temperature. White wine is served with lighter meals, such as chicken or fish. It is served chilled.

1. When is wine served in your house?

_____

2. When are the grapes picked?

_____

3. What weather is best for excellent wine?

_____

4. Is all wine made by wine-producing companies?

_____

5. What does *ferment* mean?

_____

6. What changes the sugar in the grapes into alcohol and carbon dioxide?

_____

7. How is the wine cleaned of particles?

_____

8. Which is aged longer, fine wine or table wine?

_____

9. What kind of wine is served with turkey?

_____

10. Which wine is best when it's served cold?

_____

## Discussion Questions:

1. What country are you from? Where is it located?
2. What products are grown in your country?
3. What minerals are mined in your country?
4. What goods are manufactured in your country?
5. What kinds of animals are raised in your country?
6. What products are imported into your country?
7. What products are exported from your country?

# Grammar Summary

**Active:** Farmers **grow** grapes in California.
**Passive:** Grapes **are grown** in California.
Grapes **are grown** (by farmers) in California.

Look at the above examples. Notice the word order. In the active, the object is **grapes.** In the passive, the subject is **grapes.**

## Statements:

| | | | |
|---|---|---|---|
| Cotton<br>Aerospace equipment | is | grown | in California. |
| Grapes<br>Computers | are | manufactured | in Texas. |

## Wh Questions:

| | |
|---|---|
| Where is cotton **grown**? | In Texas. |
| Where are computers **manufactured**? | In California. |
| What **is grown** in California? | Grapes are. |

# THE SEVEN WONDERS

## Past Passive

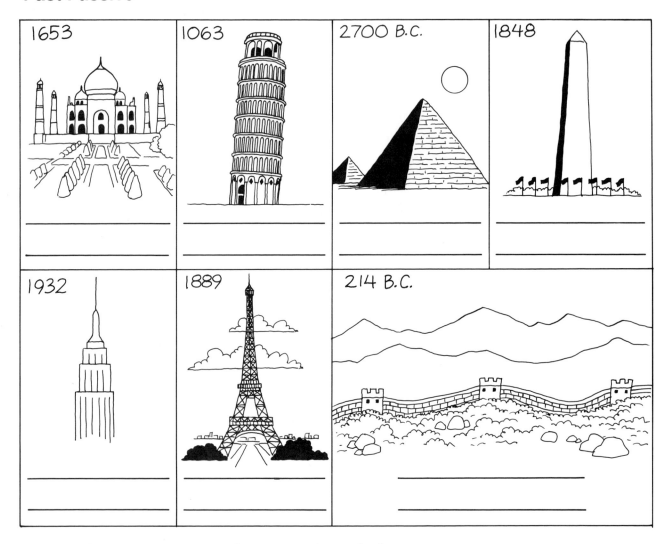

**A.** Write the correct structure and country under each picture.

| Structure | Country |
|---|---|
| Great Wall | the United States |
| Washington Monument | Egypt |
| Empire State Building | Italy |
| pyramids | China |
| Leaning Tower of Pisa | France |
| Taj Mahal | India |
| Eiffel Tower | |

**B.** Read each fact. Which structure does it describe?

**Example:** They were used as tombs for Egyptian kings.
　　　　　The pyramids.

1. They are located on the Nile River.
2. It was built to protect China from its enemies, the Mongols.
3. This structure was built to honor the 100th anniversary of the French Revolution.
4. It was constructed as a bell tower.
5. It was constructed by the king to honor his wife, Mumtaz Mahal.
6. It was built to honor the first president of the United States.
7. All parts of this iron structure were pre-made and then put together like a puzzle.
8. It is used as an office building.
9. It is surrounded by beautiful pools and gardens.
10. These structures are made of stone.

**C.** Answer these questions about the seven structures.

**Example:** When was the Empire State Building constructed?
　　　　　**It was constructed in 1932.**

1. Where are the pyramids located?
2. When were they built?
3. What were they used as?
4. When was the Great Wall built?
5. Why was it constructed?
6. Where is the Leaning Tower of Pisa located?
7. What was it first used as?
8. What year was the Taj Mahal built?
9. Why was it constructed?
10. When was the Washington Monument built?
11. What material is the Eiffel Tower made of?
12. When was the Empire State Building constructed?

**D.** Circle the correct verb in each sentence.

1. The pyramids **built** / **were built** by slaves.
2. Slaves **built** / **were built** the pyramids.
3. The Taj Mahal **surrounds** / **is surrounded** by beautiful pools and gardens.
4. Beautiful pools and gardens **surround** / **is surrounded** the Taj Mahal.
5. Workers **built** / **were built** the Empire State Building in 1932.
6. The Empire State Building **built** / **was built** in 1932.
7. The Egyptian kings **used** / **were used** the pyramids as tombs.
8. The pyramids **used** / **were used** as tombs.
9. The Eiffel Tower **made** / **was made** of iron.
10. Workers **made** / **was made** the Eiffel Tower of iron.

**E.** Combine these statements, using **which.**

**Example:** The pyramids were tombs for Egyptian kings.

which

T~~hey~~ were built more than 4,000 years ago.

The pyramids, <u>which were built more than 4,000 years ago,</u> were tombs for Egyptian kings.

1. The pyramids are located in Egypt. They were built by slaves.

2. The Empire State Building is 1,472 feet high. It was once the tallest building in the world.

3. The Empire State Building is located in New York City. It is used as an office building.

4. The Leaning Tower of Pisa was built next to a church. It was constructed as a bell tower.

5. The Leaning Tower of Pisa leans 17 feet from the vertical. It is eight stories high.

6. The Taj Mahal is located in India. It was built in 1648.

7. The Taj Mahal is the most beautiful tomb in the world. It was built in honor of Mumtaz Mahal.

8. The Great Wall extends 1,500 miles. It is twenty to thirty feet high.

9. The Great Wall was built in 214 B.C. It was constructed to protect China from its enemies.

10. The Eiffel Tower is located in Paris. It was built to honor the 100th anniversary of the French Revolution.

## Writing

**A.** Complete these sentences with the correct form of the verb. Some of the sentences are past, others are present.

| build | locate | put | surround | visit |
| construct | make | send | use | |

1. The Taj Mahal *is located* in India.

2. It _____ by beautiful pools and gardens.

3. Every year it _____ by thousands of tourists.

4. The pyramids _____ over 4,000 years ago.

5. The pyramids _____ as tombs for Egyptian kings.

6. The pyramids _____ by slaves.

7. The parts of the Eiffel Tower _____ in another city.

8. The pieces _____ to Paris.

9. Then, they _____ together like a giant puzzle.

10. The tower _____ in 1889.

146

**B.** Complete these sentences with the correct form of the verb in parentheses. Some of the sentences are active, others are passive.

1. (locate)  The Taj Mahal _is located_ in India.

2. (love)  The emperor greatly _____ his wife.

3. (die)  She _____ in 1631, giving birth to her fourteenth child.

4. (build)  The Taj Mahal _____ in her honor.

5. (finish)  The building _____ in 1653.

6. (locate)  The Great Wall _____ in China.

7. (begin)  The construction _____ in 214 B.C.

8. (make)  It _____ of stone and brick.

9. (have)  The Great Wall _____ thousands of small towers.

10. (extend)  The Great Wall _____ 1,500 miles.

**C.** Use this chart. Write questions and answers about the structures.

| When<br>Where<br>Why | was<br><br>were | the pyramids<br>the Great Wall<br>the Taj Mahal<br>the Washington Monument<br>the Eiffel Tower | built?<br>constructed? |
|---|---|---|---|

1. _Why was the Taj Mahal built?_
   _It was built to honor Mumtaz Mahal._

2. _____

3. _____

4. _____

5. _____

6. _____

7. _____

_____

8. _____

_____

9. _____

_____

10. _____

_____

**D.** Read this story about the pyramids. Then, answer the questions.

Some of the oldest structures in the world today are the pyramids, which are located in Egypt near the Nile River.

Thousands of years ago, the Egyptians believed in life after death. After a person died, the body was dried, wrapped in cloth, and made into a mummy. The mummy was placed into a coffin, which was put inside an underground tomb. Clothing, food, drink, weapons, and other personal possessions were also buried with the body. The ancient Egyptians believed that the spirit of the dead person would need them in the next life.

Great pyramids were built on the surface to honor the Egyptian kings. These four-sided structures were made of huge limestone rocks cut from mountains in southern Egypt and floated 700 miles up the Nile River. These rocks, which weighed from two to ten tons, were pulled over the land from the river and up the side of the pyramid and then set in place. The work was done by slaves, who used only ropes and ramps. Even though only simple cutting tools were used, the stones fit so tightly together that there were no spaces between the stones.

Many pyramids still stand today. The largest pyramid is called the Great Pyramid. It was built for King Cheops. It covers 13 acres and is about 481 feet high. Over 100,000 slaves worked for 20 years to build this giant structure.

1. According to the ancient Egyptians, what happened after a person died?

_____

2. What did they do with the king's body?

_____

3. Was the mummy placed above ground or under ground?

_____

4. Why were food and belongings buried with the body?

_____

5. What are the pyramids made of?

_____

6. Where was this limestone found?

_____

7. How was it taken to the site of the pyramids?

_____

8. How did the slaves move the rocks from the river to the pyramids?

_____

9. Are all of the pyramids still standing?

_____

10. How long did it take to build the Great Pyramid?

_____

## Grammar Summary

**Active:**   Workers **built** the Empire State Building in 1932.
**Passive:**  The Empire State Building **was built** in 1932.

Look at the above examples. Notice the word order. In the active, the object is **the Empire State Building.** In the passive, the subject is **the Empire State Building.**

### Statements:

| | | | |
|---|---|---|---|
| The Great Wall | was | built | in China. in 214 B.C. |
| The pyramids | were | constructed | in Egypt. four thousand years ago. |

### Wh Questions:

| | |
|---|---|
| Where **was** the Great Wall **built**? | In China. |
| When **was** it **built**? | In 214 B.C. |
| Why **was** it **built**? | To protect China from its enemies. |

# TEACHER TEXTS

The following teacher texts accompany Exercise A in many units in this book. The teacher reads the text in a clear, natural voice while the students look at the accompanying picture(s) in the unit. This is often the first introduction the students have to a structure. The teacher answers questions about grammar or vocabulary. After the students listen to the text several times, they retell any of the information they remember. Then, the class continues with the exercises in the unit.

## ◼️ UNIT 1 ◼️
## THE CLASS  Present Continuous with Who

A. Look at the picture and listen to your teacher talk about the class. Write the correct name for each picture. After you listen twice, talk about each person.

1. Toshi is wearing headphones and listening to rock music.
2. Françoise is drinking a soda.
3. Azra and Ravi are sleeping.
4. Mario is reading his dictionary.
5. Roberto is bouncing a basketball.
6. Marie is putting her homework on the desk.
7. Harry is sitting under the clock.
8. Tina is standing with Marie at the teacher's desk.
9. Ana and Paulo are coming in late.
10. Jorge is wearing a baseball uniform.
11. Celio is wearing a baseball cap and is writing on the blackboard.
12. Katarina is sitting by the window.

## ◼️ UNIT 2 ◼️
## THE DIVORCE  Future Going to

A. Look at the pictures and listen to your teacher talk about Amy and Tom's divorce. After you listen two or three times, retell the story.

1. Tom and Amy are going to get a divorce.
2. Tom is leaving tomorrow. He's going to move to another town.
3. He's going to rent an apartment there.
4. Amy is going to keep the house. The children, Carly and Tyrone, are going to live with her.
5. The children are going to visit their father once a month. They are going to live with him in July and August.
6. Tom is going to pay alimony and child support.
7. Tom and Amy are going to divide their savings.
8. Amy is going to get a job.
9. Amy is also going to study accounting part-time in the evenings.

# THE HEAD NURSE  Simple Present

**A.** Patty is the head nurse at General Hospital. Look at the pictures and listen to your teacher read about her daily routine. After you listen two or three times, retell the information.

1. Patty is the head nurse on the fourth floor at General Hospital.

2. When she first comes into the hospital, she looks in on her patients and checks their IVs.

3. The night nurse leaves Patty her report on tape.

4. Patty listens to the tape and writes her assignments.

5. Then she reads the doctors' orders on the patients' charts and gives them their medications.

6. Patty assigns duties to the four nurses who work on the fourth floor. She supervises their work.

7. The nurses wash the patients and make the beds in the morning.

8. They feed some of the patients at lunchtime.

9. They take the patients' temperature and blood pressure.

# THE JEWELRY STORE  Present with Before and After

**A.** Look at the pictures and listen to your teacher talk about Lee. Lee owns a small jewelry store in the Waterside Shopping Center. Before the customers arrive, he has many things to do. After you listen two or three times, retell the story.

1. First, Lee rolls up the iron gate. After he rolls up the iron gate, he turns off the alarm.

2. Then, he unlocks the door. After he unlocks the door, he enters the store.

3. Next, Lee turns on the radio. After he turns on the radio, he makes a pot of coffee.

4. Then, his employees, Linda and Karen, arrive. After they arrive, they unlock the storage cabinets, take out the jewelry, and display it.

5. Then, Lee takes the money out of the safe. After Lee takes the money out of the safe, he puts it into the cash register.

6. Finally, Lee puts the Open sign on the door. After he puts the Open sign on the door, the customers walk in.

Now, go back and look at the pictures again. We can talk about these pictures another way.

1. Before Lee turns off the alarm, he rolls up the iron gate.

2. Before he enters the store, he unlocks the door.

3. Before Lee makes a pot of coffee, he turns on the radio.

4. Before Linda and Karen take out the jewelry, they unlock the cabinets.

5. Before Lee puts the money into the cash register, he takes it out of the safe.

6. Before the customers walk in, Lee puts the Open sign on the door.

# COLONIAL TIMES Past

**A.** Look at the pairs of pictures. Listen to your teacher talk about life in Colonial times and life today. After you listen two or three times, retell the information.

1. Colonial people didn't shop at supermarkets. They grew their own vegetables.
2. Colonial people didn't buy milk. They milked their own cows.
3. Colonial people didn't have cars. They had horses and wagons.
4. Colonial women didn't cook on stoves. They cooked over open fires.
5. Colonial homes didn't have electricity. They had candles for light.
6. Colonial people didn't have telephones. They wrote letters to people who lived far away.
7. Colonial families didn't watch television. They read to each other.
8. Colonial children didn't study in large modern schools. They studied in one-room schoolhouses.
9. Colonial people didn't sleep on mattresses and box springs. They slept on feather beds.
10. Colonial people didn't buy clothes at big department stores. They made their own clothes.

# THE ROBBERY Past, Simple Time Clauses

**A.** Look at the pictures and listen to your teacher tell the story about the robbery at Lee's jewelry store. After you listen two or three times, retell the story.

1. This is Spike. Spike's a burglar, and tonight he tried to rob a jewelry store.
2. Spike's girlfriend, Tina, drove him to the jewelry store. She stayed in the car and watched for the police.
3. Before Spike got out of the car, he put on black gloves, a mask, and a black hat.
4. Spike walked around to the side of the store. He broke a window with a bat.
5. After Spike broke the window, he climbed into the store.
6. As soon as Spike stepped onto the floor, an alarm rang.
7. He quickly grabbed some diamonds and a pearl necklace and put them into his bag.
8. After he picked up the bag of jewelry, he jumped out of the window.
9. When he got out of the store, he heard a police siren.
10. As soon as he saw the police car, he began to run.
11. When the police saw him, they chased him down an alley.
12. Before Spike could climb over the wall, the police grabbed his foot.
13. When Tina tried to drive away, another police car blocked her car.
14. After the police caught Spike and Tina, they handcuffed them and read them their rights.
15. The police put Spike and Tina into the police car and drove them to the police station.

## UNIT 7

# THE ACCIDENT  Past Continuous

**A.** Look at the pictures and listen to your teacher describe this accident. After you listen two or three times, retell the story.

1. Lee was driving his van along Central Avenue. While he was driving home from work, he was listening to the radio. He wasn't wearing his seatbelt.

2. Lee decided to change the station. He was looking at the radio, so he wasn't paying attention to the light.

3. The light changed from green to yellow. Then, it changed from yellow to red. Lee looked up and saw that the light was red. He tried to stop, but he couldn't.

4. Olga was driving down Main Street to the store. She was wearing her seatbelt. Her children, Kathy and Jeff, were sitting in the back seat. They were wearing their seatbelts, too. Everyone was talking while they were going to the store.

5. Olga looked at the light. It turned green, so she continued into the intersection.

6. Lee hit the side of Olga's car. Thankfully, no one was hurt. The van only had a few scratches, but Olga's car had a lot of damage. A tow truck towed it away. The police gave Lee a ticket. Ellen was standing on the corner when she saw the accident. She was a witness to the accident.

## UNIT 8

# THE APARTMENT  Comparative and Superlative Adjectives

**A.** Look at the pictures of two apartment buildings. Listen to your teacher, and fill in the comparative adjective. Use the adjectives from the box.

| | | |
|---|---|---|
| expensive | cheap | dangerous |
| convenient | clean | safe |
| new | high | tall |

1. Michael and Patty's building is <u>newer</u> than Ali's building.

2. Ali's rent is <u>cheaper than</u> Michael and Patty's rent.

3. Michael and Patty's rent is <u>higher than</u> Ali's rent.

4. Michael and Patty's apartment is <u>more expensive than</u> Ali's.

5. Ali's neighborhood is <u>more dangerous than</u> Michael and Patty's.

6. Ali's building is <u>more convenient than</u> Michael and Patty's.

7. Michael and Patty's neighborhood is <u>cleaner than</u> Ali's neighborhood.

8. Michael and Patty's neighborhood is <u>safer than</u> Ali's neighborhood.

9. Michael and Patty's building is <u>taller</u> than Ali's building.

10. Michael and Patty's neighborhood is <u>less convenient than</u> Ali's neighborhood.

## ■ UNIT 10 ■
# DRIVING  Must/Have to

A. Teresa needs a car to get to her part-time job, but she needs to get a driver's license. Look at the chart and listen to your teacher talk about the many things Teresa must do in order to get a license. After you listen two or three times, retell the information.

1. First, Teresa must take a written test and a vision test.

2. The test is given in 12 languages. There are thirty questions on the test.

3. Teresa must get 80% on the written test, and she must pass the vision test in order to get a permit.

4. In order to get a permit, Teresa must pay $5.00 and show proof of her age.

5. To prove her age, she has to show her birth certificate, her alien registration card, or her passport.

6. After she gets a permit, she may take the road test.

7. When she goes to take the road test, she must have a licensed driver in the car with her.

8. She also must have auto insurance, a car, and a permit.

9. She has to pass the road test in order to get her license.

## ■ UNIT 11 ■
# COLLEGE LIFE  Present Perfect with For and Since

A. Listen to your teacher talk about three students at Kentucky State College. After you listen two or three times, retell the information.

1. Gina has been at Kentucky State for one year.

2. She has studied engineering since she began.

3. She has lived in the college dorm for a year.

4. She has worked part-time at the school cafeteria since September.

5. Her boyfriend is at another college. She has written him a lot of letters.

6. Joe has been at college for two years.

7. He has attended business classes, but he hasn't studied hard.

8. He has failed a lot of tests since September.

9. He has lived in an apartment off campus for two years.

10. He's worked at the school radio station since he started college.

11. Melissa has been at Kentucky State for three years.

12. She's studied theology since her sophomore year.

13. She has lived in the dorm for three years.

14. She's worked at the college library since her first year at college.

15. She's volunteered at the local homeless shelter since September.

# THE NEW PARENTS Future Time Clauses

**A.** Susan and Paul are expecting their first baby. Look at the pictures and listen to your teacher talk about their plans. After you listen two or three times, retell the story.

1. As soon as Susan's labor pains start, she will call the doctor.
2. When they go to the hospital, Paul will carry her suitcase.
3. After the baby is born, the nurse will put him in the nursery.
4. Before they leave the hospital, Paul will take a lot of photographs.
5. While they are in the hospital, the doctor will check the baby.
6. If the baby has a problem, the doctor will talk to Paul and Susan.
7. When they leave the hospital, they will take their presents home.
8. After they get home, Susan will take a long nap.
9. She will sleep until the baby cries.
10. Susan will feed the baby when he cries.
11. She'll call her mother if she needs help.
12. She'll stay home from work until the baby is one year old.

# THE GRANDMOTHERS Should

**A.** Susan and Paul just had a baby boy. Their mothers are thrilled with their new grandson. They are giving Susan and Paul a lot of advice, but they have different opinions about everything. Look at the pictures and listen to your teacher talk about the pictures. After you listen two or three times, retell Helen and Carol's opinions.

1. Helen thinks they should name the baby Steven.
2. Carol thinks they should name the baby Paul, after his father.
3. Helen thinks Susan should go back to work in three months.
4. Carol thinks Susan should stay home for a year.
5. Helen thinks they should bottle-feed the baby.
6. Carol thinks Susan should nurse the baby.
7. Helen thinks they should feed the baby when he cries.
8. Carol thinks they should feed the baby every four hours.
9. Helen thinks they should use disposable diapers.
10. Carol thinks they should use cloth diapers.
11. Helen thinks the baby should sleep in his own bedroom.
12. Carol thinks the baby should sleep in their bedroom.
13. Helen thinks they should pick up the baby every time he cries.
14. Carol thinks they shouldn't pick up the baby every time he cries.
15. Helen thinks the baby shouldn't wear shoes.
16. Carol thinks the baby should wear shoes.
17. Helen thinks they should give the baby a pacifier.
18. Carol thinks they shouldn't give the baby a pacifier.

## ■ UNIT 18 ■
## COLLEGE  Infinitives

**A.** Teresa wants to go to college, but she doesn't have enough money. Listen to your teacher read these sentences about her plans. Each sentence has a verb that is followed by an infinitive. Fill in the infinitive form. Then, draw a box around the first verb.

**Example:** Teresa ⟨can't afford⟩ to go to college.

1. Her parents can't afford to give her enough money.
2. Teresa managed to save some money.
3. She still needed to borrow some more.
4. She decided to get a loan from a bank.
5. She didn't expect to receive the loan.
6. She waited to hear from the bank.
7. The bank agreed to give her a student loan.
8. She decided to accept the loan.
9. She promised to pay back the loan within ten years.
10. Her grandmother offered to buy her books.

## ■ UNIT 19 ■
## A CHANGED MAN  Gerunds

**A.** Listen to your teacher read these sentences about Spike. He robbed a jewelry store and is now in jail. Each sentence has a verb that is followed by a gerund. Fill in the gerund form. Then, draw a circle around the first verb.

1. Spike can't stand being behind bars.
2. He misses being with his friends.
3. He keeps hoping to get early parole.
4. He hates eating prison food.
5. He appreciates receiving mail.
6. Spike avoids getting into trouble.
7. He anticipates getting out soon.
8. Spike admitted breaking into the jewelry store.
9. He regrets listening to his friends.
10. He is considering giving up his life of crime.

# VERBS

| verb | past | participle |
|------|------|------------|
| be | was, were | been |
| become | became | become |
| begin | began | begun |
| break | broke | broken |
| bring | brought | brought |
| build | built | built |
| buy | bought | bought |
| catch | caught | caught |
| come | came | come |
| cut | cut | cut |
| do | did | done |
| drink | drank | drunk |
| drive | drove | driven |
| eat | ate | eaten |
| fall | fell | fallen |
| feed | fed | fed |
| feel | felt | felt |
| find | found | found |
| get | got | gotten |
| give | gave | given |
| go | went | gone |
| grow | grew | grown |
| have | had | had |
| hear | heard | heard |
| hit | hit | hit |
| hold | held | held |
| hurt | hurt | hurt |
| keep | kept | kept |
| know | knew | known |
| lead | led | led |
| leave | left | left |
| make | made | made |
| pay | paid | paid |
| put | put | put |
| quit | quit | quit |
| read | read | read |
| ride | rode | ridden |
| ring | rang | rung |
| run | ran | ran |
| say | said | said |
| see | saw | seen |
| sell | sold | sold |
| send | sent | sent |

| verb | past | participle |
| --- | --- | --- |
| set | set | set |
| sing | sang | sung |
| sit | sat | sat |
| sleep | slept | slept |
| speak | spoke | spoken |
| spend | spent | spent |
| stand | stood | stood |
| steal | stole | stolen |
| sweep | swept | swept |
| take | took | taken |
| teach | taught | taught |
| tell | told | told |
| think | thought | thought |
| throw | threw | thrown |
| write | wrote | written |

# Infinitives

These verbs are followed by an infinitive.

| | | |
|---|---|---|
| afford | intend | promise |
| agree | like | try |
| arrange | manage | volunteer |
| decide | need | wait |
| expect | offer | want |
| hope | plan | would like |

# Gerunds

These verbs are followed by a gerund.

| | | |
|---|---|---|
| admit | enjoy | quit |
| anticipate | finish | recommend |
| appreciate | keep | regret |
| avoid | miss | think about |
| consider | practice | tired of |

# Infinitives or Gerunds

These verbs are followed by an infinitive or a gerund.

| | | | |
|---|---|---|---|
| begin | continue | like | start |
| can't stand | hate | love | |